Fifth International Workshop on Emoji Understanding and Applications in Social Media (Emoji 2022)

Online
14 July 2022

ISBN: 978-1-7138-5631-3

Printed from e-media with permission by:

Curran Associates, Inc.
57 Morehouse Lane
Red Hook, NY 12571

Some format issues inherent in the e-media version may also appear in this print version.

Association for Computational Linguistics
209 N. Eighth Street
Stroudsburg, Pennsylvania 18360

Phone: 1-570-476-8006
Fax: 1-570-476-0860

acl@aclweb.org

Additional copies of this publication are available from:

Curran Associates, Inc.
57 Morehouse Lane
Red Hook, NY 12571 USA
Phone: 845-758-0400
Fax: 845-758-2633
Email: curran@proceedings.com
Web: www.proceedings.com

Emoji2022 2022

The Fifth International Workshop on Emoji Understanding and Applications in Social Media

Proceedings of the Workshop

July 14, 2022

Organizing Committee

General Chair

Sanjaya Wijeratne, None

Program Chairs

Jennifer Lee, Emojination, USA
Horacio Saggion, Department of Information and Communication Technologies, Universitat Pompeu Fabra, Spain
Amit Sheth, Artificial Intelligence Institute, University of South Carolina, USA

Publication Chair

Sanjaya Wijeratne, None

Program Committee

Senior Program Committee

Sanjaya Wijeratne, None
Horacio Saggion, Universitat Pompeu Fabra, Spain

Program Committee

Lakshika Balasuriya, Gracenote, Inc., USA
Zhenpeng Chen, Peking University, China
João Cunha, University of Coimbra, Portugal
Laurie Feldman, University at Albany - State University of New York, USA
Yunhe Feng, Universtiy of Washington, USA
Dimuthu Gamage, Google, USA
Manas Gaur, Samsung Research America, USA
Jing Ge-Stadnyk, University of California, Berkeley, USA
Kalpa Gunaratna, Samsung Research America, USA
Susan Herring, Indiana University - Bloomington, USA
Anurag Illendula, New York University, USA
Xuan Lu, University of Michigan, USA
Seda Mut, Universitat Pompeu Fabra, Spain
Swati Padhee, Wright State University, USA
Sujan Perera, Amazon, USA
Alexander Robertson, Google, USA
Sashank Santhanam, University of North Carolina at Charlotte, USA
Ning Xie, Amazon, USA

Keynote Speakers

Alexander Robertson, Google, USA
Benjamin Weissman, Rensselaer Polytechnic Institute, USA

Table of Contents

Program

Thursday, July 14, 2022

09:00 - 09:10 *Welcome and Opening Remarks*

09:10 - 10:10 *Keynote - The Next 5000 Years of Emoji Research, Alexander Robertson, Google, USA*

10:10 - 10:30 *Session A - Paper Presentations*

Interpreting Emoji with Emoji
Jens Reelfs, Timon Mohaupt, Sandipan Sikdar, Markus Strohmaier and Oliver Hohlfeld

10:30 - 11:00 *Morning Break*

11:00 - 12:30 *Session B - Paper Presentations*

Understanding the Sarcastic Nature of Emojis with SarcOji
Vandita Grover and Hema Banati

Investigating the Influence of Users Personality on the Ambiguous Emoji Perception
Olga Iarygina

Beyond emojis: an insight into the IKON language
Laura Meloni, Phimolporn Hitmeangsong, Bernhard Appelhaus, Edgar Walthert and Cesco Reale

Graphicon Evolution on the Chinese Social Media Platform BiliBili
Yiqiong Zhang, Susan Herring and Suifu Gan

Conducting Cross-Cultural Research on COVID-19 Memes
Jing Ge-Stadnyk and Lusha Sa

12:30 - 14:00 *Lunch Break*

14:00 - 15:00 *Keynote - Processing Emoji in Real-Time, Benjamin Weissman, Rensselaer Polytechnic Institute, USA*

Thursday, July 14, 2022 (continued)

15:00 - 15:45 *Session C - Paper Presentations*

EmojiCloud: a Tool for Emoji Cloud Visualization
Yunhe Feng, Cheng Guo, Bingbing Wen, Peng Sun, Yufei Yue and Dingwen Tao

Semantic Congruency Facilitates Memory for Emojis
Andriana Ge-Christofalos, Laurie Feldman and Heather Sheridan

Emoji semantics/pragmatics: investigating commitment and lying
Benjamin Weissman

15:45 - 15:50 *Closing Remarks*

Interpreting Emoji with Emoji: ⛱ ⇒ ☀️ 😎 🌊

Jens Helge Reelfs[1], Timon Mohaupt*[2], Sandipan Sikdar[3], Markus Strohmaier[4], Oliver Hohlfeld[1]
[1] Brandenburg University of Technology, [2] Talentschmiede Unternehmensberatung AG
[3] RWTH Aachen University, [4] University of Mannheim, GESIS, CSH Vienna
reelfs@b-tu.de, timon.mohaupt@me.com, sandipan.sikdar@cssh.rwth-aachen.de, markus.strohmaier@uni-mannheim.de, hohlfeld@b-tu.de

Abstract

We study the extent to which emoji can be used to add interpretability to embeddings of text and emoji. To do so, we extend the POLAR-framework that transforms word embeddings to interpretable counterparts and apply it to word-emoji embeddings trained on four years of messaging data from the Jodel social network. We devise a crowdsourced human judgement experiment to study six use-cases, evaluating against words only, what role emoji can play in adding interpretability to word embeddings. That is, we use a revised POLAR approach interpreting words and emoji with words, emoji or both according to human judgement. We find statistically significant trends demonstrating that emoji can be used to interpret other emoji very well.

1 Introduction

Word embeddings create a vector-space representation in which words with a similar meaning are in close proximity. Existing approaches to make embeddings interpretable, e.g., via contextual (Subramanian et al., 2018), sparse embeddings (Panigrahi et al., 2019), or learned (Senel et al., 2018) transformations (Mathew et al., 2020)—all focus on text only. Yet, emoji are widely used in casual communication, e.g., Online Social Networks (OSN), and are known to extend textual expressiveness, demonstrated to benefit, e.g., sentiment analysis (Novak et al., 2015; Hu et al., 2017).

Goal. We raise the question if we can leverage the expressiveness of emoji to make word embeddings—and thus also emoji—interpretable. I.e., can we adopt word embedding interpretability via leveraging semantic polar opposites (e.g., cold / hot) to emoji (e.g., ❄️ / ☀️, or 😠 / 😊) for interpreting words or emoji w.r.t. human judgement.

*Timon Mohaupt performed this work during his master thesis at Brandenburg University of Technology and RWTH Aachen University.

Approach. Motivated and based upon POLAR (Mathew et al., 2020), we deploy a revised variant POLAR$^\rho$ that transforms arbitrary word embeddings into interpretable counterparts. The key idea is to leverage semantic differentials as a psychometric tool to align embedded *terms* on a scale between two polar opposites. Employing a projection-based transformation in POLAR$^\rho$, we provide embedding dimensions with semantic information. I.e., the resulting interpretable embedding space values directly estimate a *term*'s position on a-priori provided polar opposite scales, while approximately preserving in-embedding structures (§ 2).

The main contribution of this work is the large-scale application of this approach to a social media corpus and especially its evaluation in a crowdsourced human judgement experiment. For studying the role of emoji in interpretability, we create a word-emoji input embedding from on a large social media corpus. The dataset comprises four years of complete data in a single country from the online social network provider Jodel (48M posts of which 11M contain emoji). For subsequent main evaluation, we make this embedding interpretable with word and emoji opposites by deploying our adopted tool POLAR$^\rho$ (§ 3).

Given different expressiveness of emoji, we ask **RQ1)** How does adding emoji to POLAR$^\rho$ impact interpretability w.r.t. to human judgement? I.e., do humans agree on best interpretable dimensions for describing words or emoji with word or emoji opposites? And **RQ2)** How well do POLAR$^\rho$-semantic dimensions reflect a *term*'s position on a scale between word or emoji polar opposites?

Human judgement. We design a crowdsourced human judgement experiment (§ 4) to study if adding emoji to word embeddings and POLAR$^\rho$ in particular increases the interpretability—while also answering how to describe emoji best. Our human judgement experiment involves six campaigns explaining *Words* (W/*) or *Emoji* (E/*) with *Words*,

Proceedings of the The Fifth International Workshop on Emoji Understanding and Applications in Social Media, pages 1 - 10
July 14, 2022

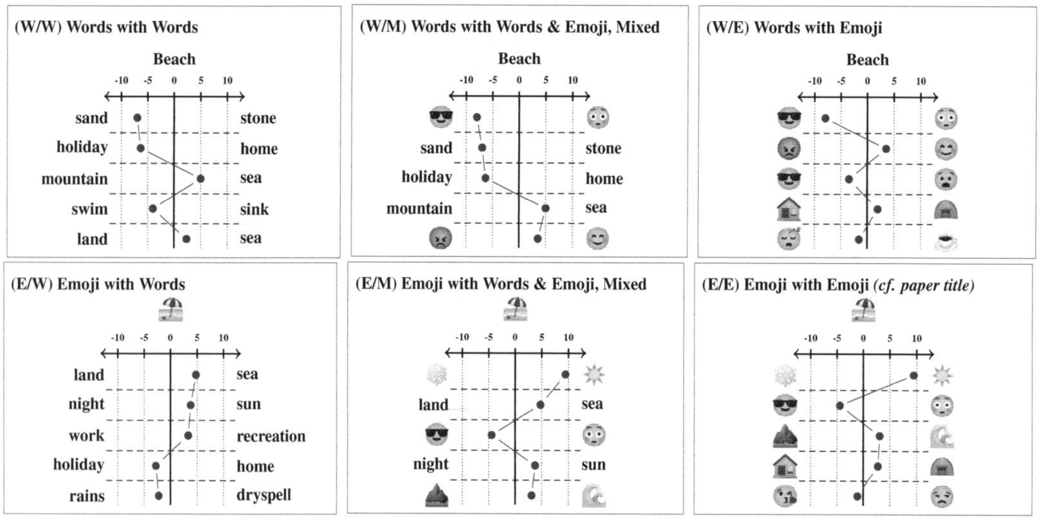

Figure 1: The POLAR-framework (Mathew et al., 2020) makes word embeddings interpretable leveraging polar opposites. It provides a new interpretable embedding subspace with systematic polar opposite scales: Along six use-cases, we evaluate which role emoji expressiveness plays in adding interpretability to word embeddings. I.e., how well can our adopted POLAR$^\rho$ interpret (W/*) words or (E/*) emoji with words, emoji or both (*/M), *Mixed*. We test POLAR$^\rho$ alignment with human judgement as represented in shown semantic profiles above.

Emoji, or both *Mixed*. We evaluate two test conditions to answer both research questions: *(RQ1)* a *selection* test studies if human subjects agree to the POLAR$^\rho$ identified differentials (e.g., how do emoji affect POLAR$^\rho$ interpretability?), and *(RQ2)* a *preference* test that studies if the direction on a given differential scale is in line with human judgement (e.g., how well does POLAR$^\rho$ interpret scales).

Results. POLAR$^\rho$ identifies the best interpretable opposites for describing emoji with emoji, yet generally aligning well with human judgement. Except interpreting words with emoji only probably due to lack of emoji expressiveness indicated by coder agreement. Further, POLAR$^\rho$ estimates an embedded *terms*' position on a scale between opposites successfully, especially for interpreting emoji.

Broader application. Not all emoji have a universally agreed on meaning. Prior work showed that differences in the meaning of emoji exist between cultures (Guntuku et al., 2019; Gupta et al., 2021). Even within the same culture, ambiguity and double meanings of emoji exist (Reelfs et al., 2020). Currently, no data-driven approach exists to infer the meaning of emoji—to make them interpretable. Our proposed approach can be used to tackle this challenge since it makes emoji interpretable.

2 Creating Interpretable Embeddings

We explain next our deployed tool for creating interpretable word-emoji embeddings: POLAR (Mathew et al., 2020); and provide detail on a revised POLAR extension via projection.

2.1 POLAR Approach

Semantic Differentials. Based upon the idea of semantic differentials as a psychometric tool to align a word on a scale between two polar opposites (Fig. 1), POLAR (Mathew et al., 2020) takes a word embedding as input and creates a new interpretable embedding on a polar subspace. This subspace, i.e., the opposites used for the interpretable embedding are defined by an external source.

That is, starting with a corpus and its vocabulary $\mathcal{V}$, a word embedding created by an algorithm a (e.g., Word2Vec or GloVe) assigns vectors $\overrightarrow{\mathbb{W}^a_v} \in \mathbb{R}^d$ on d dimensions to all words $v \in \mathcal{V}$ according to an optimization function (usually word co-occurrence). This pretraining results in an embedding $\mathbb{D} = \left[\overrightarrow{\mathbb{W}^a_v}, v \in \mathcal{V}\right] \in \mathbb{R}^{|\mathcal{V}| \times d}$.

Such embedding spaces carry a semantic structure between embedded words, whereas the dimensions do not have any specific meaning. However, we can leverage the semantic structure between words to transform the embedding space to carrying over meaning into the dimensions: POLAR uses N semantic differentials/opposites that are itself items within the embedding, i.e., $\mathbb{P} = \left\{(p^i_z, p^i_{-z}), i \in [1..N], (p^i_z, p^i_{-z}) \subseteq \mathcal{V}^2\right\}$.

As shown in Fig. 2a, given two anchor points for each polar opposite, a line between them represents a differential—which we name POLAR direction

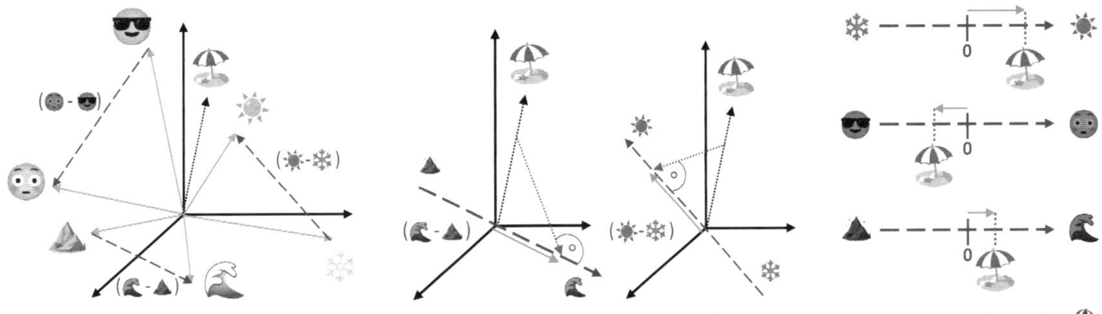

(a) Polar Directions/Differentials. (b) Excerpt: Per Direction Orthogonal Projection. (c) Interpretable Scales for ⛱️.

Figure 2: POLAR (Mathew et al., 2020) with Projection in a nutshell: We showcase POLAR$^\rho$ interpreting emoji with emoji (E/E) (cf. paper title). *(a)* We leverage polar opposites (*here:* ❄️/☀️, 😎/😳, ⛰️/🌊) to provide embedding dimensions with semantic information. By using opposite differential directions (red dashed vectors), we create a new interpretable subspace. *(b)* Orthogonal projection (blue dotted vectors) of an embedded term (*here:* ⛱️) onto this subspace (e.g., *left:* ⛰️/🌊, *right:* ❄️/☀️) yields a direct scale measure between both opposites in the adjacent leg (green vectors, directed alike the differential). *(c)* The resulting interpretable embedding now contains a tangible position estimation along employed polar dimensions for each embedded term (*here:* ⛱️).

(red dashed vectors):

$$\overrightarrow{dir_i} = \overrightarrow{\mathbb{W}^a_{p^i_z}} - \overrightarrow{\mathbb{W}^a_{p^i_{-z}}} \in \mathbb{R}^d$$

Base Change. Naturally, we can use these differentials as a new basis for the interpretable embedding $\mathbb{E}$. Gathering all directions in a matrix $dir \in R^{N \times d}$, we obtain for all embedded *terms* $v \in \mathcal{V}$: $dir^T \overrightarrow{\mathbb{E}_v} = \overrightarrow{\mathbb{W}^a_v}$, and ultimately apply a base change transformation $\overrightarrow{\mathbb{E}_v} = (dir^T)^{-1} \overrightarrow{\mathbb{W}^a_v}$ yielding an interpretable subspace along the differentials $\overrightarrow{dir_i}$ that carries over specific geometric semantics from the input embedding. I.e., for each word $v \in \mathcal{V}$ within the resulting interpretable embedding $\mathbb{E}$, its embedding vector $\overrightarrow{\mathbb{E}_v}$ now carries a measure along each polar dimension's semantics.

Limitations. Polar opposites being very close in the original embedding space might tear apart. From a technical perspective, the used pseudo inverse for the base change becomes numerically ill-conditioned if $d \approx N$ (Mathew et al., 2020).

2.2 POLAR$^\rho$ Extension: Projection

While the base change approach seems natural, its given limitations lead us to propose a variant that comes with several benefits. Instead of creating a new interpretable vector space, we take measurements on the differentials dir defined as before (Fig. 2a, red dashed vectors). However, we now project each embedding vector $\overrightarrow{\mathbb{W}_v}$ for v orthogonally onto the differentials as shown in Fig. 2b (blue dotted vectors). This leads to a smallest distance between both lines w.r.t. the differential, yet simultaneously allows for a direct scale measure on the differential vector as shown in Fig. 2b & Fig. 2c (green vectors). Thereby, we also *decouple* the transformation matrix, which eases later add-ins to the interpretable embedding.

Orthogonal projection (blue dotted vectors) of each input embedding vector $\overrightarrow{\mathbb{W}^a_v}$ onto a differential i provides us the adjacent leg vector as follows:

$$\text{oproj}_{dir_i}(\overrightarrow{\mathbb{W}^a_v}) = \underbrace{\frac{\overrightarrow{\mathbb{W}^a_v} \cdot \overrightarrow{dir_i}}{|\overrightarrow{dir_i}|}}_{scalar} \cdot \underbrace{\frac{\overrightarrow{dir_i}}{|\overrightarrow{dir_i}|}}_{direction}$$

As this adjacent leg (green vectors)'s direction naturally equals the differential, we focus only on the scalar part representing a direct scale measure. By normalizing the differential vector lengths $\hat{dir} = dir \cdot |dir|^{-1}$, the projected scale value conveniently results in: $\text{oproj}^{scalar}_{dir_i}(\overrightarrow{\mathbb{W}^a_v}) = \overrightarrow{\mathbb{W}^a_v} \cdot \overrightarrow{\hat{dir}_i}$.

This transformation allows to create a new interpretable embedding $\mathbb{E} \in \mathbb{R}^{|\mathcal{V}| \times N}$ for each embedding vector $\overrightarrow{\mathbb{W}^a_v}$ (exemplified in Fig. 1) as follows:

$$\overrightarrow{\mathbb{E}_v} = \text{oproj}^{scalar}_{dir}(\overrightarrow{\mathbb{W}^a_v}) = \hat{dir}^T \overrightarrow{\mathbb{W}^a_v} \in \mathbb{R}^N$$

Computationally it requires an inital matrix multiplication for each embedded *term*; Dimension increments require a dot product on each *term*.

Downstream Tasks. Other experiments indicate POLAR$^\rho$ downstream task performance being on par with the input embedding, and an edge over base change POLAR if $d \approx N$ (not shown).

2.3 Measuring Dimension Importance

There can be many possible POLAR dimensions, which requires to select the most suitable ones.

That is, we want to define a limited set of opposites that best describes words or emoji w.r.t. interpretability across the whole embedding.

Extremal Word Score (EWSO). We propose a new metric to measure the quality of polar dimensions complementing heuristics from (Mathew et al., 2020). It measures the embedding confidence and consistency along available differentials. The idea of POLAR$^\rho$ is that directions represent semantics within the input embedding. We determine embedded *terms* shortest distance to these axes via orthogonal projection; we use resulting intersections as the position w.r.t. the directions.

That is, as a new heuristic, for each of our differentials dir_i, we look out for $k = 10$ embedded words at the extremes (having the highest scores in each direction) and take their average cosine distance within the original embedding $\mathbb{D}$ to the differential as a measure. This results in the average similarity of existing *extremal* words on our scale—a heuristic that represents the skew-whiffiness within the extremes on a differential scale.

3 Approach: Embedding & Polarization

We next propose an approach to improve the interpretability of word embeddings by adding emoji. It uses our extended version POLAR$^\rho$ and adds emoji to the POLAR space by creating word embeddings that include emoji.

3.1 Data Set

We create a word embedding out of a social media text corpus, since emoji are prominent in communication within Online Social Networks. We decided to use a corpus from the Jodel network, where about one out of four sentences contain emoji (see (Reelfs et al., 2020)).

The Jodel Network. We base our study on a country-wide complete dataset of posts in the online social network Jodel, a mobile-only messaging application. It is location-based and establishes local communities relative to the users' location. Within these communities, users can *anonymously* post photos from the camera app or content of up to 250 characters length, i.e., microblogging, and reply to posts forming discussion threads.

Corpus. The network operators provided us with data of content created in Germany from 2014 to 2017. It contains 48M sentences, of which 11M contain emoji (1.76 emoji per sentence on average).

Ethics. The dataset contains no personal information and cannot be used to personally identify users except for data that they willingly have posted on the platform. We synchronize with the Jodel operator on analyses we perform on their data.

3.2 Semantic Differential Sources

POLAR$^\rho$ can create interpretable embeddings w.r.t. a-priori provided opposites. We next describe how we select these opposites to make POLAR$^\rho$ applicable to our data. Most importantly, the approach requires being part of or locating desired opposites within the original embedding space.

Words. As we extend the word embedding space with emoji, we still want to use words. We find common sources of polar opposites in antonym wordlists (Shwartz et al., 2017) as used in the original POLAR work. To fit our German dataset, we translated and manually checked all pairs keeping 1275 items. From GermaNet (Hamp and Feldweg, 1997), we extracted 1732 word pairs via antonym relations leading to $|\mathbb{P}_{\text{words}}| = 1832$ word pairs.

Emoji. Being not ideal, but due to lack of better alternatives, we ended up heuristically creating semantic opposites from emoji through qualitative surveys across friends and colleagues resulting in $|\mathbb{P}_{\text{emoji}}| = 44$ emoji pairs, cf. Tab. 3. While we could use far more opposites especially of facial emoji, due to emoji clustering in the input embedding, spanned expressive space would arguably become redundant at similar EWSO scores for many directions. Effectively it may bias interpretability over proportionally towards facial emoji.

3.3 Polarization

Preprocessing. We tokenize sentences with `spaCy` and remove stopwords. To increase amounts of available data, we remove all emoji modifiers (skin tone and gender): {👨🏾‍🌾, 👩🏻‍🌾, 👨🏿‍🌾} $\rightarrow$ 🧑‍🌾. Due to German language, we keep capitalization.

Original Embedding. We use `gensim` implementation of `Word2Vec` (W2V). A qualitative investigation suggests that skip-gram works better than CBOW (better word analogy). We kept training parameters largely at defaults including negative sampling, opting for $d = 300$ dimensions.

Interpretable Embedding. The actual application of embedding transformation is simple. We create the matrix of differentials dir, the POLAR subspace, according to our antonym-set $\mathbb{P}_{\text{words}} \cup \mathbb{P}_{\text{emoji}}$ (§ 3.2). After normalizing the subspace vectors, we create all embedding vectors via projec-

interpret	W	*with* Mixed	E
Words	(W/W)	(W/M)	(W/E)
Emoji	(E/W)	(E/M)	(E/E)

(a) Campaigns Overview. We interpret Words & Emoji with likewise Words, Emoji, and Mixed (both).

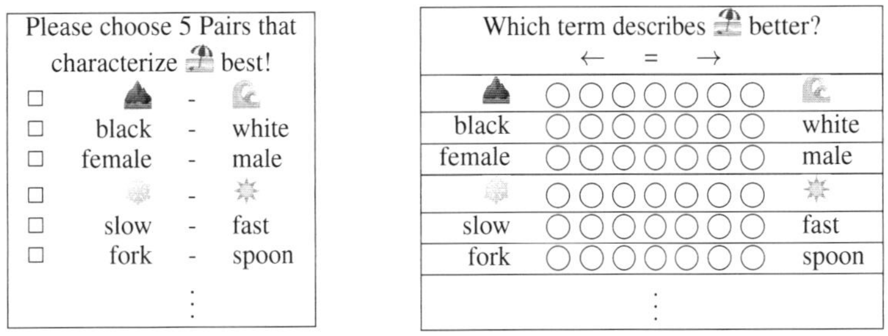

(b) Selection Task for Emoji/Mixed (E/M). (c) Preference Task for Emoji/Mixed (E/M).

Figure 3: *(a)* We conduct six campaigns measuring human interpretability for including emoji to the POLAR$^{\rho}$ embedding space. Exemplified with the Emoji Mixed campaign (E/M): interpreting emoji with emoji and words. *(b)* In the Selection test, coders choose suitable differentials for describing a given term. *(c)* In the Preference test, coders provide their interpretation of a given term to a differential scale.

tion $\overrightarrow{\mathbb{E}_v} = \hat{dir}^T \overrightarrow{\mathbb{W}_v}, \forall v \in \mathcal{V}$. Though normalization requires careful later additions to the POLAR space, we opted for standard normalization, $\mathbb{E}_{\text{stdnrm}} = [\mathbb{E} - \text{mean}(\mathbb{E})] \cdot \text{std}(\mathbb{E})^{-1}$, to ensure that the whole embedding space aligns properly around the center of gravity on each differential scale. We select the best suited opposites for a given embedding space by using the Extremal Word Score (§ 2.3) for d=500+44 dimensions (words + emoji).

4 Human Evaluation Approach

While we have now created a supposedly interpretable embedding, it remains to be seen how well it is *perceived* by humans. That is, we next evaluate our two key RQs, discuss significance, and provide further details: *RQ1)* How well does POLAR$^{\rho}$ with EWSO perform in selecting most interpretable dimensions at varying expressiveness of words and emoji? *RQ2)* How well do POLAR$^{\rho}$ scalar values reflect directions on the differential scales? *i)* Do humans prefer emoji to words? *ii)* How well do human raters align w.r.t. interpretability? *iii)* What impact do demographic factors play in interpretability with or without emoji?

4.1 Evaluation design

To gather human judgement, we employ crowdsourcing on the Microworkers platform.

4.1.1 Questions & Evaluation Metrics

Our evaluation of the POLAR$^{\rho}$ approach including emoji to the differentials bases on two main questions next to demographics.

Selection test. Analogous to the original work, we want to find out whether humans agree on best interpretability of POLAR$^{\rho}$ selected differentials with a word intrusion task. The question asks our coders to select five out of ten differentials that describe a given word best as shown in Fig. 3b. We select half of these dimensions according to the highest absolute projection scale values (most extreme). The other half consists of a random selection from the bottom half of available differentials. I.e., if the projection approach determines interpretable dimensions well, humans would choose all five out of five POLAR$^{\rho}$ chosen differentials.

As any user might choose differently, we count how often coders choose certain differentials. The resulting frequencies immediately translate in a ranking that we leverage for calculating the fraction of Top 1..5 being POLAR$^{\rho}$ chosen differentials.

Preference test. Additionally, we introduce the preference test evaluating whether the direction on a given differential scale is in line with human judgement. That is, for the same words from the selection test, we display the same ten dimensions (5 top-POLAR$^{\rho}$, 5 random bottom) where coders select their interpretation of the given word on scales as shown in Fig. 3c. Typical for semantic differential scales (Tullis and Albert, 2008; Osgood et al., 1957), we deliberately use a seven point scale representing -3 to 3, allowing more freedom than 3 or 5 points (Simms et al., 2019). Further, we specifically allow a center point—being equal—as it might indicate both being *equally well* or *not good at all.*

Due to scale usage heterogeneity (Rossi et al., 2001), we normalize coder chosen directions (shift+scale according to mean) prohibiting disproportional influence of single coders. We evaluate the coder agreement by counting direction (sign) non-/alignment with the POLAR$^{\rho}$ projection scale.

Demographics. There is a multitude of other external factors that might have impact on coders' choices. To better understand participant background, we ask for their education, emoji usage (familiarity), smartphone platform (different emoji pictograms), and if they had used Jodel before.

4.1.2 Evaluation Setup

Crowdworker Campaigns We run a campaign for each of the cross product between words only, emoji only, and mixed Tab. 3a and Fig. 2. *(W/W)* word/word sets a baseline comparison to results from the original POLAR work, albeit now using the projection approach. *(W/M)*: word/mixed uses not only words, but includes emoji to the POLAR subspace. *(W/E)*: word/emoji uses only emoji to describe words. *(E/W)*: emoji/word provides another baseline as to how well emoji may be interpreted with words only. *(E/M)*: emoji/mixed uses both, emoji and words to interpret emoji. *(E/E)*: emoji/emoji may be the most interesting as we only use the expressiveness of emoji to describe emoji.

For mixed cases (emoji and words within the POLAR subspace), we create rankings from absolute scale values on both types (words/emoji) separately and then select them equally often to achieve similar amounts of word and emoji differentials.

Used Words & Emoji. We selected 50 words and emoji to be described in each campaign. To ensure that *i)* we only use common words that are very likely known to our coders, and *ii)* these words are captured well within the underlying embedding, we pick them out of the upper 25% quantile by occurrences in the corpus ($n \geq$1.6k). I.e., we chose emoji and words that appear frequently and should therefore be well-known. For words, we ensured that they are part of the German dictionary *Duden*.

Tasks Setup. Within our six campagins, we now have each 50 emoji or 50 words to be interpreted. We bundled this into 5 tasks each consisting of 10 emoji/words—resulting in 30 different tasks. Each of these tasks contains the Selection test, Preference test, and demographics.

Subjects. Human judgement and crowdsourced evaluations are noisy by nature. While it is usually sufficient to employ few trusted expert coders, it is suggested to use more in the non-expert case (Snow et al., 2008). Thus, we assign 5 different annotators to each of the 30 tasks. At estimated 10-15min duration, we provide 3$ compensation for answering a single task, above minimum wage in our country.

Quality Assurance. Any crowdsourcing task offers an incentive to rush tasks for the money, which requires us to employ means of quality assurance (QA). As we have an uncontrolled environment and thus untrusted coders, we handcraft test questions for the selection and preference test. This task is non-trivial as we require unambiguity in *correct* answers (we ensured this with multiple qualitative tests among friends and colleagues), while simultaneously not being too obvious. We place one test question for selection and one for preference randomly into each task (ending up in 11 words or emoji per task). This also means that each coder can only participate in up to 5 different tasks within a single campaign before re-seeing a test question.

We define acceptance thresholds of four out of five correct answers for both, the selection test and the correct direction for the preference test.

4.2 Results

Within the crowdsourcing process, we rejected about 10% of all tasks according to our QA measures, which then had to be re-taken. We ended up with 6 campaigns each having 50 words/emoji answered by 5 coders; summing up to completed 150 tasks. In total, 16 different coders accomplished this series of which 4 completed $\Sigma \geq 100$ tasks.

4.2.1 Interpreting Emoji

First we focus on the describing emoji campaigns (E/*). We present our main evaluation results in Tab. 1. Within columns, we show results for random, original POLAR, and our six campaigns. We split the rows into results from the selection test across Top1..5 entries and the preference test.

Selection Test. We find very good results along all emoji campaigns (E/*) being consistently better than any campaign describing words (W/*). The best performance was achieved for explaining emoji with emoji (E/E); others are on par.

We want to note however, that the small size of used emoji-differential set may ease selection. E.g., facial expression emoji regularly achieve higher embedding scores than others, which thus may bias the bottom control half (§ 4.1.1). However, interpreting emoji or words with words only, (E/W) and (W/W), achieve comparable performance.

Preference Test. Here, we make the same observation; The projected scales on the differentials are mostly well in line with human judgement.

4.2.2 Interpreting Words

Again, we refer to Tab. 1, but now change our focus to describing words, campaigns (W/*).

Selection Test. Albeit not being directly comparable, using POLAR$^{\rho}$ in compaings: describing

Task		Random	*POLAR*	(W/W)	(W/M)	(W/E)	(E/W)	(E/M)	(E/E)
Selection	Top 1	0.500	*0.876*	0.79	**0.83**	0.60	0.81	0.79	**0.88**
	Top 2	0.222	*0.667*	**0.62**	0.61	0.35	0.67	0.68	**0.77**
	Top 3	0.083	*0.420*	**0.45**	0.42	0.15	0.54	0.57	**0.67**
	Top 4	0.024	*0.222*	**0.30**	0.18	0.07	0.37	0.37	**0.59**
	Top 5	0.004	*0.086*	**0.14**	0.08	0.01	0.22	0.19	**0.38**
Preference		0.500	-	**0.740**	0.672	0.576	0.800	**0.848**	0.832

Table 1: Campaign results. Random & original POLAR baseline. Selection and Preference results across campaigns. Words are better described by word dimensions, and emoji are better described by emoji dimensions.

words with words (W/W), or describing words with words and emoji (W/M) achieved performance well on par with POLAR. Noteworthy, describing words with emoji (W/E) yielded the worst results. The projection scale values for the emoji dimensions were mostly lower compared to words. I.e., according to POLAR$^\rho$, for words only few emoji differentials would be among the top 5 opposites.

Preference Test. As for the preference test, describing words yield the best results using word opposites only (W/W). Explaining words with emoji (W/E) performs particularly worse.

4.2.3 Result Confidence

Significance. To test for differences within the coder alignment with POLAR$^\rho$, we model both, the selection and preference test. With our primary goal to understand the impact of including emoji to a POLAR$^\rho$ interpretable word embedding, we anchor to the (W/W) campaign as a baseline.

For the selection test, we count if coders aligned with POLAR$^\rho$ or chose any of the random alternatives across the Top 1..5 selection. For the preference test, we count whether coders aligned with POLAR$^\rho$'s scale direction. We apply double-sided chi-square tests χ^2 with $p < 0.05$ between the interpreting words with words (W/W) baseline and the remaining five campaigns.

We identify significant differences in coder-POLAR$^\rho$ alignment to the (W/W) baseline when describing words with emoji (W/E) over Top1..5 selection and preference. Counts from explaining emoji with emoji (E/E) signal significance for preference and selection Top3..5. Coder-POLAR$^\rho$ alignment in preferences is also significant for describing emoji with emoji and words (E/M).

4.2.4 Observations

Emoji. As a byproduct, we also show if emoji opposites are preferred over words. That is, we focus on the mixed campaigns describing words and emoji with words and emoji (*/M).

α	(W/W)	(W/M)	(W/E)	(E/W)	(E/M)	(E/E)
Selection	0.44	0.35	0.24	0.46	0.39	**0.55**
Preference	0.57	0.41	0.34	**0.61**	0.54	0.60
Preference *POLAR$^\rho$ only*	0.65	0.52	0.40	**0.70**	0.64	0.68
Preference *random only*	0.31	0.17	0.25	**0.31**	0.22	0.22

Table 2: Inter-rater agreement Krippendorff's α across campaigns. Coders achieve the best agreement in selection test of emoji-based campaigns (E/*) and generally within the preference test measuring differential scales.

We establish a baseline by filtering the counts for all non-POLAR$^\rho$ randomly chosen dimensions being word or emoji representing a Bernoulli experiment. I.e., along the random dimensions, our coders chose 228 vs. 221 and 167 vs. 187 words over emoji. Applying chi-squared statistics indicates, that both types (words and emoji) are chosen equally often at least cannot be rejected.

We next analyze the POLAR$^\rho$ chosen dimensions in the mixed campaigns. Here, coders chose words over emoji as follows: 465 vs. 336 in the (W/M), and 414 vs. 482 in the (E/M) campaign. We find statistically significant favors for words to interpret words and emoji to describe emoji.

Scale Usage. We find no evidence for any directional biases within our preference test (cf. 3c).

Coder Agreement. While the aggregate results are compelling, we use the Krippendorff-alpha metric to measure coder agreement along all six campaigns as shown Tab. 2; higher scores depict better agreement. We split the overall results by test first (Selection & Preference), but also show additional agreement results for preferences along POLAR$^\rho$ chosen dimensions and their random counterpart.

Most agreement is within the *moderate* regime. This observation does not come unexpected from our five non-expert classifiers per task. Overall, we find that coders agree better for well-performing campaigns. We identify the best agreement scores for interpreting emoji with emoji (E/E); coders agree least in the worst performing explaining words with emoji campaign (W/E).

For the preference test, we subdivide our results into POLAR$^{\rho}$ chosen differentials and compare them to the randomly chosen ones. While the agreement on the random opposites is only *fair*, the agreement on POLAR$^{\rho}$ chosen opposites is consistently better: Estimating differential scale directions via POLAR$^{\rho}$ for words yields *moderate* agreement, whereas coders consistently align *substantially* in interpreting emoji. We presume emoji may convey limited ideas, but are easier to grasp, have better readability; the campaings interpreting emoji (E/*) were generally accomplished faster.

4.2.5 Demographics

Though we are confident in applied QA measures, none of the demographics can be confirmed. The annotator sample-size is small and thus most likely not representative. Further, we find most workers providing contrasting answers across multiple tasks they participated in, rendering collected demographic information unusable.

5 Related Work

No universal meaning of emoji. Prior work showed that the interpretation of emoji varies (Miller et al., 2016; Kimura-Thollander and Kumar, 2019), also between cultures (Guntuku et al., 2019; Gupta et al., 2021). Even within the same culture, ambiguity and double meanings of emoji exist (Reelfs et al., 2020) and differences exists on the basis of an individual usage (Wiseman and Gould, 2018). These observations motivate the need to better understand the meaning of emoji. Currently, no data-driven approach exists to make emoji interpretable—a gap that we aim to close.

Interpretable *word* embeddings. Word embeddings are a common approach to capture meaning; they are a learned vector space representation of text that carries semantic relationships as distances between the embedded words. A rich body of work aims at making word embeddings interpretable, e.g., via contextual (Subramanian et al., 2018), sparse embeddings (Panigrahi et al., 2019), or learned (Senel et al., 2018) transformations (Mathew et al., 2020)—all focus on text only. Recently, (Mathew et al., 2020) proposed the POLAR that takes a word embedding as input and creates a new interpretable embedding on a polar subspace. The POLAR approach is similar to SEMCAT (Senel et al., 2018), but is based on the concept of semantic differentials (Osgood et al., 1957) for creating a polar subspace. It measures the meaning of abstract concepts by relying on opposing dimensions associated (good vs. bad, hot vs. cold, conservative vs. liberal). In this work, we extend and use POLAR.

Emoji embeddings. Few works focused on using word embeddings for creating emoji representations, e.g., (Eisner et al., 2016) or (Reelfs et al., 2020). (Barbieri et al., 2016) used a vector space skip-gram model to infer the meaning of emoji in Twitter data (Barbieri et al., 2016). Yet, the general question if the interpretability of word embeddings can be improved by adding emoji and if different meaning of emoji can be captured remains still open. In this work, we adapt the POLAR interpretability approach to emoji and study in a human subject experiment if word embeddings can be made interpretable by adding emoji and how emoji can be interpretated by emoji.

6 Conclusion

We raise the question whether we can leverage the expressiveness of emoji to make word embeddings interpretable. Thus, we use the POLAR framework (Mathew et al., 2020) that creates interpretable word embeddings through semantic differentials, polar opposites. We employ a revised POLAR$^{\rho}$ method that transforms arbitrary word embeddings to interpretable counterparts to which we added emoji. We base our evaluation on an off the shelf word-emoji embedding from a large social media corpus, resulting in an interpretable embedding based on semantic differentials, i.e., antonym lists and polar emoji opposites.

Via crowdsourced campaigns, we investigate the interpretable word-emoji embedding quality along six use-cases (cf. Fig. 1): Using word- & emoji-polar opposites (or both *Mixed*), to interpret words (W/W, W/E, W/M) and emoji (E/W, E/E, E/M), w.r.t. human interpretability. Overall, we find POLAR$^{\rho}$'s interpretations w/wo emoji being well in line with human judgement. We show that explaining emoji with emoji (E/E) works statistically significantly best, whereas describing words with emoji (W/E) systematically yields the worst performance. We also find good alignment to human judgement estimating a *term*'s position on differential scales, using the POLAR$^{\rho}$-projection.

That is, emoji can improve POLAR$^{\rho}$'s capability in identifying most interpretable semantic differentials. We have demonstrated how emoji can be used to interpret other emoji using POLAR$^{\rho}$.

Acknowledgements

We thank Felix Dommes, who was instrumental for this work by developing and implementing the POLAR$^\rho$ projection approach and the Extremal Word Score in his Master Thesis.

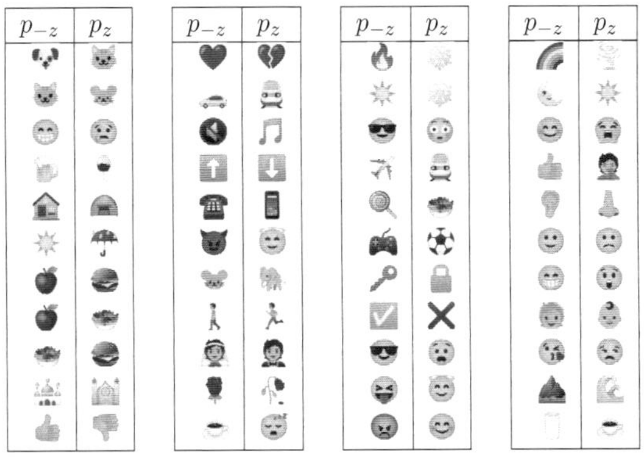

Table 3: Used heuristically identified polar emoji opposites $(p_{-z}, p_z) \in \mathbb{P}_{\text{emoji}}$. We opted for a diverse set of opposites selecting only few facial emoji differentials.

References

F. Barbieri, F. Ronzano, and H. Saggion. 2016. What does this Emoji Mean? A Vector Space Skip-Gram Model for Twitter Emojis. In *LREC*.

Ben Eisner, Tim Rocktäschel, Isabelle Augenstein, Matko Bošnjak, and Sebastian Riedel. 2016. emoji2vec: Learning emoji representations from their description. In *Proceedings of The Fourth International Workshop on Natural Language Processing for Social Media*, Austin, TX, USA. Association for Computational Linguistics.

Sharath Chandra Guntuku, Mingyang Li, Louis Tay, and Lyle H Ungar. 2019. Studying cultural differences in emoji usage across the east and the west. In *Proceedings of the International AAAI Conference on Web and Social Media*, volume 13, pages 226–235.

Mitali Gupta, Damir D Torrico, Graham Hepworth, Sally L Gras, Lydia Ong, Jeremy J Cottrell, and Frank R Dunshea. 2021. Differences in hedonic responses, facial expressions and self-reported emotions of consumers using commercial yogurts: A cross-cultural study. *Foods*, 10(6):1237.

Birgit Hamp and Helmut Feldweg. 1997. GermaNet - a lexical-semantic net for German. In *Automatic Information Extraction and Building of Lexical Semantic Resources for NLP Applications*.

T. Hu, H. Guo, H. Sun, T. T. Nguyen, and J. Luo. 2017. Spice up your chat: the intentions and sentiment effects of using emojis. In *ICWSM*.

Philippe Kimura-Thollander and Neha Kumar. 2019. Examining the "global" language of emojis: Designing for cultural representation. In *Proceedings of the 2019 CHI conference on human factors in computing systems*, pages 1–14.

Binny Mathew, Sandipan Sikdar, Florian Lemmerich, and Markus Strohmaier. 2020. The polar framework: Polar opposites enable interpretability of pre-trained word embeddings. In *WWW*, pages 1548–1558.

Hannah Miller, Jacob Thebault-Spieker, Shuo Chang, Isaac Johnson, Loren Terveen, and Brent Hecht. 2016. "blissfully happy" or "ready to fight": Varying interpretations of emoji.

P. . Novak, J. Smailović, B. Sluban, and I. Mozetič. 2015. Sentiment of emojis. *PloS one*.

C.E. Osgood, G.J. Suci, and P.H. Tannenbaum. 1957. *The Measurement of Meaning*. Illini Books, IB47. University of Illinois Press.

Abhishek Panigrahi, Harsha Vardhan Simhadri, and Chiranjib Bhattacharyya. 2019. Word2sense: sparse interpretable word embeddings. In *ACL*.

Jens Helge Reelfs, Oliver Hohlfeld, Markus Strohmaier, and Niklas Henckell. 2020. Word-emoji embeddings from large scale messaging data reflect real-world semantic associations of expressive icons. *Workshop Proceedings of the 14th International AAAI Conference on Web and Social Media*.

Peter E Rossi, Zvi Gilula, and Greg M Allenby. 2001. Overcoming scale usage heterogeneity. *Journal of the American Statistical Association*, 96(453).

Lutfi Kerem Senel, Ihsan Utlu, Veysel Yucesoy, Aykut Koc, and Tolga Cukur. 2018. Semantic structure and interpretability of word embeddings. In *IEEE/ACM TASLP*, 10.

Vered Shwartz, Enrico Santus, and Dominik Schlechtweg. 2017. Hypernyms under siege: Linguistically-motivated artillery for hypernymy detection. In *EACL*, pages 65–75.

Leonard Simms, Kerry Zelazny, Trevor Williams, and Lee Bernstein. 2019. Does the number of response options matter? psychometric perspectives using personality questionnaire data. *Psychological Assessment*, 31.

Rion Snow, Brendan O'connor, Dan Jurafsky, and Andrew Y Ng. 2008. Cheap and fast–but is it good? evaluating non-expert annotations for natural language tasks. In *EMNLP*.

Anant Subramanian, Danish Pruthi, Harsh Jhamtani, Taylor Berg-Kirkpatrick, and Eduard Hovy. 2018. Spine: Sparse interpretable neural embeddings. In *AAAI*, volume 32.

Thomas Tullis and William Albert. 2008. *Measuring the User Experience: Collecting, Analyzing, and Presenting Usability Metrics*. Morgan Kaufmann Publishers Inc., San Francisco, CA, USA.

Sarah Wiseman and Sandy JJ Gould. 2018. Repurposing emoji for personalised communication: Why means "i love you". In *Proceedings of the 2018 CHI conference on human factors in computing systems*, pages 1–10.

Beyond emojis: an insight into the IKON language

Laura Meloni[1], Phimolporn Hitmeangsong[2], Bernhard Appelhaus[3], Edgar Walthert[1], and Cesco Reale[1]

[1]KomunIKON, Neuchâtel, Switzerland
laura.meloni@komunikon.com
edgar.walthert@komunikon.com
cesco.reale@komunikon.com
[2]Institute of Psychology, University of Pécs, Hungary
phimolporn.hitmeangsong@komunikon.com
[3]Department of Linguistics. University of Bremen, Germany
bernhard@uni-bremen.de

Abstract

This paper presents a new iconic language, the IKON language, and its philosophical, linguistic, and graphical principles. We examine some case studies to highlight the semantic complexity of the visual representation of meanings. We also introduce the Iconometer test to validate our icons and their application to the medical domain, through the creation of iconic sentences.

1 Introduction

Since its introduction in the early 1970s, textual computer-mediated communication (CMC) has been enriched by visual elements that express emotion and attitude: emoticons (sideways faces typed in ASCII characters), emojis (designed, like emoticons, to facilitate emotion expression in text-based conversation, but visually richer, more iconic, and more complex), stickers (larger, more elaborate, character-driven illustrations, or animations to which text is sometimes attached) (Konrad et al., 2020).

Graphic symbols have been extensively utilized in communication all over the globe, particularly on social media and instant messaging services. More recently, studies have examined the use of emojis in other dimensions. For example, consider the usage of emojis or symbols to gauge consumer satisfaction with a product or service in the business field (Paiva, 2018). Emojis have been investigated in the medical industry to assess patients' symptoms (Bhattacharya et al., 2019). Apart from Emojis - that are not considered a language by most linguists - there are also visual languages, that were created to enable a full visual communication (e.g. Bliss, Zlango, iConji, etc.). Nonetheless, several limitations have been found in these visual communication tools. For example, some of them are based on national languages reproducing their inconsistencies and difficulties; some were conceived to be handwritten and so are very stylized and abstract; some have a too simple grammar, that does not allow sufficient precision in conveying complex meanings. The IKON language was conceived to address these limitations.

IKON allows semantic compositionality by joining icons (as in Bliss, LoCoS and Piktoperanto), the use of grammar categories (Bliss), and the consistent use of iconemes (as in VCM), high iconicity (as in AAC languages and Emoji). IKON aims to reduce abstractness and language dependency.

Our contribution has multiple aims: i) to examine IKON theoretical approach and its application to a few case studies based on semantic dimensions such as modality, verbs of motion, of perception, and of communication; ii) to present the Iconometer test, a crucial tool to understand how individuals interpret IKON language; iii) To propose an application of IKON in the medical domain through a bachelor's thesis project developed by a member of our team.

The remainder of the paper is structured as follows: section 2 briefly discusses examples of iconic languages and their semantic approach. Section 3 specifies IKON's theoretical approach. Section 4 brings a few case studies of our icons. Section 5 presents the Iconometer, the next step to evaluate the designed icons. Section 6 describes IKON sentences in the dentist-patient frame. Finally, conclusions are reported in section 7.

Proceedings of the The Fifth International Workshop on Emoji Understanding and Applications in Social Media, pages 11 - 20
July 14, 2022 ©2022 Association for Computational Linguistics

2 Semantic analysis in icon languages

Iconic languages have been used successfully in human-computer interfaces, visual programming, and human-human communication. They have, in most cases, a limited vocabulary of icons and a specific application. There are also "natural visual languages" that use logograms such as Chinese, Mayan, and Egyptian (Reale et al., 2021).

We will provide a short semantic analysis of Emojis, *Emojitaliano*, and Augmentative and Alternative Communication (AAC).

The most popular icons today are emojis, which roused discussions about to what extent they are a language and whether it is universal. Emojis are widely used to express the user's communicative intent functioning as tone marking or as a word in a verbal cluster. However, emojis lack grammatical function words and morphosyntax. In spite of that, some consider it an emergent graphical language (Ge and Herring, 2018).

Emojitaliano is an autonomous communicative Emoji code born for the Italian language. It was created for the translation of Pinocchio (2017), launched on Twitter by F. Chiusaroli, J. Monti, F. Sangati within the *Scritture Brevi* community (https://www.scritturebrevi.it/). *EmojitalianoBot* on Telegram then supported the translation project. It contains the grammar and dictionary of the iconic system. *Emojitaliano* consists of a repertoire of lexical correspondences and a grammatical structure predefined that reflects the content found in Pinocchio. It respects linguistic principles such as linearity, economy, and arbitrariness. *Emojitaliano* does not have a high degree of iconicity (similarity between form and meaning of a sign) because many solutions are the result of an idiomatic or culturally marked decision not related to human experiences (Nobili, 2018). For example, *emojitaliano* represents the abstract concept of *guilt* with man + woman + apple, representing the referent using a biblical and culture-specific metaphor.

The field of (AAC) has created various technologies to facilitate communication for people who cannot communicate through language in the standard way. Different approaches exist to develop AAC iconic languages. From the semantic point of view, these systems developed three ways to represent language: i) single meaning pictures ii) alphabet-based methods are often subdivided to include spelling, word prediction, and orthographic word selection iii) semantic compaction uses multi-meaning icons in sequences to represent language. Minspeak, for example, uses semantic compaction (Albacete et al., 1998; Tenny, 2016). Non-linear AAC has been proposed based on semantic roles and verb valency (Patel et al., 2004).

Figure 1: *We dual inclusive icon* (I-You). It is obtained from the *I* pronoun (1.P.SG singular) (left) and *You* pronoun (2. SG) (right).

The attention of researchers now focuses on the automatic detection of icons' meaning, using machine learning and word embedding techniques (Ai et al., 2017). Nevertheless, in the creation of a visual language, it is also essential to empirically assess the degree of polysemy of a given icon, how its meaning is conveyed according to different levels of knowledge of users, evaluating the ambiguity within the system (Dessus and Peraya, 2005; Tijus et al., 2007).

3 Creation of an icon in IKON

3.1 Methodology

IKON follows philosophical, linguistic, and graphical principles. IKON language aims to create a compositional, iconic, international, and language-independent system (see Reale et al., 2021 for a more detailed analysis).

3.1.1 Philosphical framework

The philosphical framework determines the principles and values at the core of the project. It then informs both linguistic principles (e.g., by using hyperonymic form to have a transcultual icon as in Figure 5 or representing semantically different concepts by different icons for language independence), and graphical guidelines (e.g., grey as skin color as in the icons presented below).

IKON is human-centered. In designing a concept or undefined events, generic humans are preferably used as participants, creating a similarity between the sign and our human experience.

IKON intends to be iconic and intelligible so as to be easily understandable by people of different backgrounds. That is, taking into account different cultural and geographic realities creating transcultural icons. Pictographic, highly iconic representations are favoured, while abstract symbols are used only when no better alternative is identified, or when it is already widely used (e.g. road signs).

IKON system aims to be inclusive, representing specific identities through the use of no discriminating symbols or generalization (e.g. specific icons and symbols commonly used to represent various genders), or by using unspecified and identity-neutral icons specified in the graphic guidelines.

3.1.2 Linguistic principles

Linguistic principles involve different linguistic dimensions: semantics, grammar and morphology, syntax.

The IKON lexicon is a core set of around 500 icons covering basic concepts, used directly to communicate complex ideas and, indirectly, as "building blocks" to create new "compound words" (Reale et al., 2021). As we will see, the list is continuously growing as from each meaning other meanings stem, if necessary, in a disambiguating process. For instance, from a typological point of view, there are languages that show more granularity than English within the number system. This is revealed the most in the pronoun system (Corbett, 2000). The dual inclusive pronoun - used to refer strictly to two people including the speaker - can be found all over the world and in different language families. It is common in Austronesian languages (e.g., in Māori *tāua* 'I and you') but also found in Upper Sorbian, a West Slavonic language (*mój* 'we two') (Corbett, 2000). In light of that, we decided to create an icon to represent the dual inclusive pronoun by using the icons for the pronouns *I* (first person singular) and *you* (second singular person) as shown in Figure 1.

IKON considers polysemy. Each semantically different concept found in our path has a different icon (e.g., to smell can mean "to produce smell" or "to perceive smell", and we decided to create two different icons for those meanings). Moreover, the main sense of a word is preferred, because a more specialized, metaphorical, or idiomatic sense is often culturally specific (e.g., *to go away* is represented within its literal motion sense and does not involve other idiomatic usages such as *stop bothering someone*, *leave someone alone*. In this way, language independence - a crucial value of our philosphical framework - is increased.

At this point, we use a linear word order reflecting the linear syntax of natural spoken languages. However, as previously mentioned, more flexible syntactic orders and even a bi-dimensional syntax are conceivable.

3.1.3 Compositional rules

A graphical-semantic interface accounts for a finite number of pictorial forms so as to assure coherence of the system. We go from the simplest icons to the compound icons.

Pictographic icons. When possible, icons are pictographic, that is a prototypical (Rosch et al., 1976; Croft et al., 2004) and conventional type of an item (e.g., the most telling representation of a window).

Abstract symbol. Sometimes an abstract symbol is used if it is widespread and more comprehensible (e.g., traffic signs).

Contextual icons. Some concepts and items might be easily recognized if represented within a given context. This kind of representation is called "contextual". Contextual icons are built as visual scenes with several elements: graphic markers (such as arrows, circles, and color oppositions) pointing to one specific sub-element of the whole picture. In this case, what is highlighted is what it means.

Compound icons are more complex from a semantic point of view, obtaining meaning through various strategies:

Juxtaposition. Simple juxtaposition of two or more elements, which seems the emergent use of emojis (Ge and Herring, 2018).

Contrastive form. Sometimes a meaning is better understood in opposition to another meaning (e.g., *day* as contrasted to *night* with yes-no symbols to signal the intended meaning).

Hyperonymic icons. As complex as they seem, serve to understand complex concepts as a set of different but related elements.

Hyponymic icons. Hyponymic icons, on the opposite, highlight a specific member of the hyperonymic set. Ancient and modern visual systems present these strategies (Reale et al., 2021).

3.1.4 Linguistic resources

The preset forms and strategies described above enable a flexible framework that allows us to graphically encode meanings according to the analysis of semantic, semiotic and cultural needs. For a practical example see Figure 5 (Hyperonymic icon for *to thank*). Individuating the semantic frame of a lexical unit (Fillmore and Baker, 2010) - the core elements of a word meaning - is particularly essential if disambiguation of meanings is needed.

When it comes to verbs, it is also important to assess the semantic types and thematic role in the argument structure to include the appropriate participants and frames in the related icon. Most lexical resources contain a large amount of linguistic information that can be exploited: Wordnet (Miller, 1998) (semantic lexicon with definitions and lexical relations), FrameNet (Boas, 2005) (offers an extended amount of semantic and syntactic phrase specifications), Sketch Engine (Kilgarriff et al., 2014) (a multilanguage annotated corpora resource). A limitation is that Wordnet and FrameNet are implemented only for the English language. However, they are becoming available in other languages. Other multilingual resources are also growing (Boas, 2005; Baisa et al., 2016). Thus, a more typological approach is needed and recommended to confirm hypotheses with respect also to our theoretical approach.

3.1.5 Graphic guidelines

The graphical guidelines are the the visible part of our project. For the most part they visually reflect the linguistic principles, and the philosophical framework, but also influence them due to graphic constraints. The main points are:

Vectorial. Readable at 30 px and at 4000 + px (vectorial).

Text-Free. In general, the text is avoided as much as possible, to keep language independence. There can be exceptions: letters, brands, proper names, sentences/words about phonetics, or linguistics.

Background Independent. No background is applied to the icons unless it is meaningful.

Colors. Palette of 24 colors and Black-and-White. Each icon exists also in black and white. To keep icons racially neutral, we use gray as skin color.

Pixel Perfect. All icons are aimed to be pixel-perfect on 48 by 48 pixels; diagonal lines are at slopes 1:1, 1:2, 1:3, or 1:6.

Arrows and lines. Arrows are purple, normally used to show one object inside one scene: solid arrows for emphasis; dashed arrows for movement. Lines dividing the two or more scenes are dotted lines, usually horizontal or vertical. Except when another angle makes more sense or is more practical.

Contrastive Icons. The contrast between 2 scenes is expressed by default through small symbols "yes-no" (green V or red X); the contrast between more than 2 scenes is expressed by default by graying out (or crossing out) the contrastive scenes and circling the signified scene.

Figure 2: Initially proposed icons for the modal verb *must*.

In the following sections, we present a few case studies, providing concrete examples of the process and semantic considerations that precede the design of complex concepts.

4 Case studies

A semantic criterion, namely the inherent conceptual content of the event, is used to group meanings and relative icons

4.1 Modality

Initially, the symbol of a traffic policeman in the position of giving instruction was proposed to express the modal verb *must* (Figure 2 (a)). Another option was an obligatory road signaled with a red arrow - an idea inspired by the nobel pasigraphy (figure 2 (b)). However, these icons did not seem intuitive enough.

The World Atlas of Language Structure Online (WALS) provided typological information to analyze how modality (situational and epistemic) is realized cross-linguistically. *Must* can be used to express epistemic modality - a proposition is necessarily true - or situational modality - a situation of obligation in which the addressee's action (e.g., going home) is essential i.e., necessary. The following analysis is focused on the latter. *Must* can be decomposed in terms of the speaker's intention, in the sense of the speech acts theory. The intention we focus on is the "speaker directives" (illocutionary force) which correspond to concepts like "obligation", or "advice".

Non-verbal communication is a source of visual language. A pointing gesture is a movement toward some region of space produced to direct attention to that region. Scholars suggest that pointing remains a basilar communicative tool throughout the lifespan, deployed across cultures and settings, in both spoken and signed communication (Clark,

Figure 3: Proposal for *must* based on the index-finger gesture.

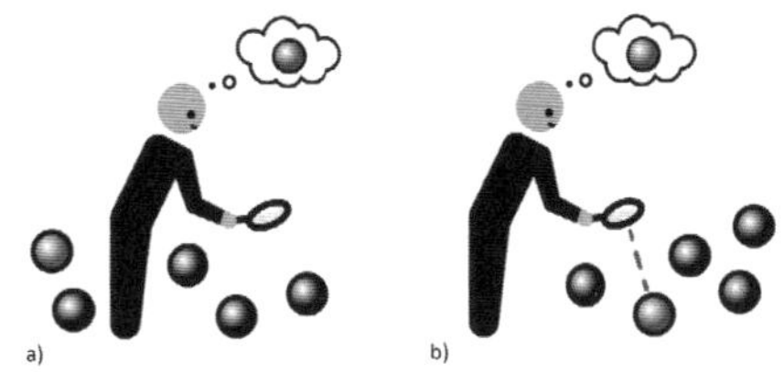

Figure 4: Icon for *to search* (a) and icon for *to find* (b).

2003; Camaioni et al., 2004). The communicative role of hand gestures is evident in the fact that hand-based emojis are the third most used type of emoji (Gawne and Daniel, 2021). However, there is limited literature on the diversity of forms and meanings, causing the exclusion of new culturally motivated encodings (Gawne and Daniel, 2021). To our knowledge, there are no studies focused on the use of index finger or hand pointing to express the abstract linguistic category of modality here discussed. Nevertheless, studies on Chinese and English metaphors suggest this possibility. As a matter of fact, in Chinese, the metaphors TO GUIDE OR DIRECT IS TO POINT WITH A FINGER and THE POINTING FINGER STANDS FOR GUIDANCE OR DIRECTION are linguistically manifested. That is, compounds and idioms involving zhǐ 'finger' express the metaphors above (among others) such as *zhǐ-shì* (finger pointing–show) 'indicate; point out; instruct; directive; instruction; indication', *zhǐ-dǎo* (finger pointing–guide) 'guide; direct; supervise; advice; coach'. These abstract senses related to performative language, guiding, directing, and advising here have a bodily root (Yu, 2000). Concerning the emblematic open hand gesture shaped in various forms, these are shared across regions and recognized as the verbal message to stop (Matsumoto and Hwang, 2013).

Finally, we hypothesize that the index finger pointing can be an indexical non-deictic gesture that has a general emphasis function in the dialogue (Allwood et al., 2007), which serves to give emphasis to the speaker saying in a dialogue. This allows the expression of the obligation and the necessity of an object or event. We developed the icons shown in Figure 3. The initial idea of an officer giving orders remained. The position of the index finger is up at 45 degrees (not encoded in emoji). The next step will be to test these versions against other proposals (Figure 2 or traffic signs-based icons).

4.2 Verbs of perception

According to Wordnet (Miller, 1998), *to find* and *to search* are perceptual verbs in the sense of becoming aware and establishing the existence of an object through the senses. These verbs are in a non-factive causal relation because *to search* MAY cause *to find* (Ježek, 2016). Searching for something has the purpose to find it even if one does not necessarily achieve the intended goal. To find indicates the result of discovering what that person is seeking. Therefore, we developed two similar icons (Figure 4). We chose to employ a magnifying glass to symbolize the process of searching and finding, following the practice of user interfaces of computers, smartphones, or websites. Payuk and Zakrimal (2020) defined the magnifying glass symbol as "finding and searching without any character or letter." It also signals the feature to zoom in and out on software or programs installed on a device (Ferreira et al., 2005). Both icons use a purple ball, which depicts an abstract object (often used in IKON) that a person is looking for or has found and that they have in mind, among other abstract objects (gray balls). This permits the distinction between *searching* and *finding*.

4.3 Verb of communication

As for words denoting communicative content, *to thank* is a verb of particular interest. There are many different ways for people all around the world to express gratitude or show appreciation to one another. Having analyzed the most widespread gestures used to thank, it was evident that there was no single gesture widespread enough to be understood across the world. For this reason, we decided to encode the cultural variation of thanking using a hyperonymic strategy shown in Figure 5. Using body language and hand gestures we depict the concept of thanking in its different cultural forms. The hyperonymic icon merges four scenarios: a person holding a hand on the chest, a common gesture for gratitude across cultures, referring to the

Figure 5: Hyperonymic icon for *to thank.*

Figure 6: Icon for the motion verb *to go*.

widespread metaphorical association of the heart as a container of emotions (Gutiérrez Pérez, 2008); the formal handshake gesture; a person bowing and the hand-folded gesture, commonly used to greet and pay respect in South Asia and Southeast Asia.

4.4 Verb of motion

Wilkins and Hill (1995) define the verb *to go* as referring to a motion-away-from-the-speaker or motion-not-toward-speaker. IKON represents the verb *to go*, as shown in Figure 6, in its general meaning: a person moving toward a direction, signaled by the dashed purple arrow (following the graphic guidelines described above (Sect. 3.1.5). (2005) described the semantics of the arrow graphic. The arrow has three slots including a tail, body, and head. If a person's image or icon is behind the tail is able to interpret that a person moves toward somewhere or someone. However, it is vice versa if it is put in the front of the head of an arrow. That should be something or someone moving toward a person.

Languages lexicalize the various types of motion in different ways. For example, Russian motion verbs differ from English or Italian in how they lexicalize direction of movement (unidirectional or in the sense of back and forth but not limited to that) and means of transportation ('go-on-foot' or 'go-by-vehicle'). Figure 6 represents the general meaning of movement toward an unknown destination. Nevertheless, we can have specific icons that encode direction, type of motion, and path.

5 Iconometer test

Iconometer is a software developed by the Univ. of Geneva (Peraya et al., 1999) to implement the theoretical approach proposed by Leclercq (1992) to assess the degree of polysemy of a visual representation (icon, diagram, figurative image, photograph) and measure its adequacy to its prescribed meaning.

Iconometer was previously used within the IKON language to evaluate icons from the family domain and gender symbols used to signify gender. (Reale et al., 2021). Family icons representing family relationships with different gender signifiers were tested: only gender symbols, only haircuts, or both gender signifiers. The results demonstrated no significant difference in accuracy or certainty when comparing gender symbols, haircuts, or the combined gender signifiers. The research contributed in two ways: i) IKON language makes use of gender signifiers; ii) few family icons were subject to reconsideration due to low certainty in the test (e.g., grandfather misunderstood for stepfather).

Our current objective is to compare the level of certainty that participants had on interpretations of icons in different domains: family, modality (e.g., icons for *must* and *can*), operators, contrastive icons, motion verbs. In some cases, we proposed two or more versions of the same icon; in others, only a single version was displayed to assess how it was perceived. The new Iconometer test presents the participant with 30 visual images and no text. Below the images are 8 possible meanings and the option to write a personal answer.

The participant must distribute a total of 100 points among the different meanings according to certainty. The participant must give the most points to the meaning that seems most certain and has the option to give 100 points to a single meaning.

Currently, we have not yet a sufficient population to draw conclusions and we leave the discussion of results and consideration about the mechanism of meaning assignment for future work.

6 IKON in context: the medical domain

To get a useful set of iconic vocabulary for a typical emergency dental treatment situation, a set of questions and sentences that are important in the anamnesis and treatment of patients were developed, e.g., questions about previous illnesses of various organs, diabetes, or medication allergies. The aim was to design unique pictograms in the

Figure 7: The iconic sentence *Do you have toothache with cold or hot food and drinks?*

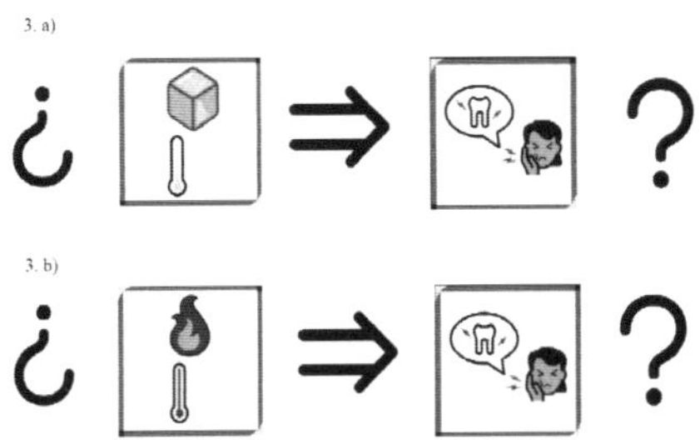

Figure 8: The simpler iconic sentence *Does cold cause your toothache? Does hot cause your toothache?*

style of IKON accomplished with the help of a graphic designer and suggestions from providers of free pictograms on the internet.

The development of intuitive content is shown using the example of the question sentence: *Do you have a toothache with hot or cold food or drinks?* (Figure 7). The concept of contrastive representation in a pictogram, like above for hot and cold, is certainly helpful in isolated observation. However, grasping this principle and paying attention to the form requires an additional cognitive effort, thus creating possibilities for misinterpretation. In this context, it seems redundant. Also, the icons for eating and drinking seem redundant and confusing.

The *and/or* sign also caused difficulties for some respondents. In light of that, it is easier to construct an iconic sentence that does not follow the syntax of questions formulated in the modern Indo-European languages of Europe. Accordingly, Figure 8 shows the same question being split into two sentences with a simplified syntax.

6.1 Online survey

An online survey with the help of Google forms was conducted to verify the thesis of simplification and to be able to make a statement about the comprehensibility of iconic sentences and signs. The subjects selected were of different age groups and cultural backgrounds. The subjects were 52: 40 Germans, 3 non-German Europeans, 4 Asians, 3

Iconic sentences or icon	Correct answers	Rating scale (1=certain, 5=very uncertain)
Pregnancy	98%	1.94
The tooth is destroyed, I will remove it.	94%	2.1
Heart	90%	2.54
Fever	90%	2.25
Open your mouth	88%	2.08
Endodontic treatment	83%	2.43
Dental filling	81%	2.64
Are your lungs ok?	69%	1.94
Do you take medications on a regular basis?	69%	2.62
Do you have an allergy to medicines?	65%	2.51
I'll give you an anesthetic, so you won't be in pain.	63%	2.71
Diabetes	62%	2.82
Do you have a toothache on pressure / on cold?	60%	-
Dental x-ray	54%	2.96
Where do you have toothache?	38%	-
Since when you had toothache?	38%	2.76
You have a dental abscess, I will cut/open.	33%	3.18
Average understanding rate of individual pictograms (8x)	81%	
Average understanding rate of sentences (9x)	59%	

Table 1: Percentages of correct answers and degree of certainty on comprehension of single icons and iconic sentences were in the survey.

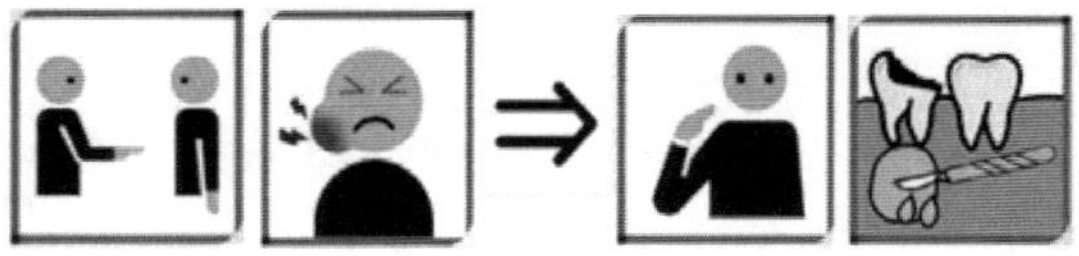

Figure 9: Iconic sentence for *You have dental abscess, I will cut to get the pus out.*

Figure 10: Version A and version B of the iconic sentence *Since when you have tootache?*

Africans, 2 Mexicans. The age ranged from 15-30 years (30 subjects), 31-50 (8 subjects) and over 50 (14 subjects). The sample is unfortunately quite unbalanced as there were great difficulty in recruiting people for the survey in countries where we have no personal contacts. The original plan was to survey 20 people from each of 5 continents.

The younger group consisted mainly of university students, the older group were mostly personal contacts, who met the requirements of the study; overall, it can be assumed that the participants have an above-average level of education, although we did not collect any data on this in the survey. However, all participants spoke at least another language in addition to their native language, showing a further indicator of an above-average educational level of the test persons. Due to the small number of cases and the uneven distribution of subjects by age group and origin, the results of the survey can only be seen as a pilot study for further research. It is easier to evaluate an online survey when options have to be ticked according to the multiple-choice method. On the other hand, it is not easy to find plausible alternative meanings with complete sentences. Thus, participants had to write their solutions following a more reliable approach. This method is the opposite of the Iconometer test discussed in section 5. In terms of age, size of place of residence and use of emojis, the study showed the following trends: the group 31-50 years got the best results, no significant difference between the 15-30 and the >50 group exists; the smaller the city in which the tester live, the better the result, suggesting that the degree of graphical stimuli in bigger places does not have a significant relevance; in contrast to the intuitive thesis that users of emojis have a better comprehension rate, the frequent use of emojis as a pictorial method of communication does not lead to a better comprehension of the icons. Due to the small number of cases and the uneven distribution of the test persons in terms of age groups and origin, these results only serve as a pilot study for further research.

The answers were 69% correct, but there were great differences. Table 1 reports the percentages of correct answers for each icon or iconic sentence. Overall, single pictograms were 81% correct, while sentences were 59% correct. Single icons for *pregnancy, fever, heart, open the mouth* and the sentence *the tooth is broken, I will remove it* were correctly identified 90% of the time. The sentence *You have a dental abscess, so I will cut to get the pus out* had the worst result with 33% (Figure 9), perhaps due to the very specific medical treatment. The complex sentence involving time *since when you have toothache?* created difficulties (Figure 10. For this question two versions were proposed: 70% of participants preferred version B, which conveys the core elements of the meaning (e.g., pronouns had been considered confusing by participants). Only 38% answered correctly. Overall, it was read as *appointment at the dentist.*

Generally, the difference in comprehensibility rate was found much greater between the different icons and sentences than between the groups. The future task will be to work on semantic and syntactic concepts, especially in whole sentences, where the comprehension rate is still insufficient. In a clinical situation of patient-dentist discourse with a language barrier, the icons would be only part of the communication. Body language, pointing gestures, sounds, and demonstration material helps facilitate comprehension.

7 Conclusions

In this work, we presented the IKON language with a core set of about 500 core concepts. New meanings are semantically analyzed and then translated into a visual representation. In this process, IKON follows defined criteria that assure coherence and flexibility within the system while continuously growing its vocabulary. We examined concepts grouped according to the conceptual event encoded, such as modality (e.g., *must*), perception, motion, communication verbs. These are complex events or subject to cultural variation. Their examination gave an insight into the semantic analysis required to design a visual correspondent: from the understanding of the semantic frame of a word (description of a type of event, relation, entity, participants) to semiotic and non-verbal language analysis. We then introduced modern linguistic resources that can be helpful for their depiction. However, only testing the different icons will tell us which one performs best among speakers of different backgrounds. Positively, cultural variation plays a significant role in our work, and IKON aims at giving equal representation.

We presented the Iconometer test, previously used to test the family icons and gender signifiers. The test is essential to assess the adequacy of the prescribed icons. The new test is ongoing as we do not have a sufficient diversified population yet. Therefore, we plan to analyze and discuss results in future work and review icons that do not perform well on the test.

Finally, we brought an example of the IKON language application in the dentist-patient discourse showing that medical content can be transferred successfully into an iconic language. Building iconic sentences is possible and beneficial, in that helps people with language impairment or in a situation of linguistic barrier to communicate in such a complex domain as healthcare. However, the study demonstrated that semantic considerations adopted for a single icon may not work in a more complex syntax because of the cognitive effort required.

Aknowledgments

The authors address special thanks to the graphic designers of KomunIkon for the production of the shown icons, Esteban Quiñones and Esteban Bahamonde for their support on the Iconometer software, Marwan Kilani and Linda Sanvido for their precious suggestions.

References

Wei Ai, Xuan Lu, Xuanzhe Liu, Ning Wang, Gang Huang, and Qiaozhu Mei. 2017. Untangling emoji popularity through semantic embeddings. In *Proceedings of the International AAAI Conference on Web and Social Media*, volume 11, pages 2–11.

Patricia L Albacete, Shi-Kuo Chang, and Giuseppe Polese. 1998. Iconic language design for people with significant speech and multiple impairments. *Assistive Technology and Artificial Intelligence*, pages 12–32.

Jens Allwood, Loredana Cerrato, Kristiina Jokinen, Costanza Navarretta, and Patrizia Paggio. 2007. The mumin coding scheme for the annotation of feedback, turn management and sequencing phenomena. *Language Resources and Evaluation*, 41(3):273–287.

Vít Baisa, Jan Michelfeit, Marek Medveď, and Miloš Jakubíček. 2016. European Union language resources in Sketch Engine. In *Proceedings of the Tenth International Conference on Language Resources and Evaluation (LREC'16)*, pages 2799–2803, Portorož, Slovenia. European Language Resources Association (ELRA).

Sudip Bhattacharya, Amarjeet Singh, and Roy Rillera Marzo. 2019. Delivering emoji/icon-based universal health education messages through smartphones. *AIMS Public Health*, 6(3):242.

Hans C Boas. 2005. Semantic frames as interlingual representations for multilingual lexical databases. *International Journal of Lexicography*, 18(4):445–478.

Luigia Camaioni, Paola Perucchini, Francesca Bellagamba, and Cristina Colonnesi. 2004. The role of declarative pointing in developing a theory of mind. *Infancy*, 5(3):291–308.

Francesca Chiusaroli, Johanna Monti, and Federico Sangati. 2017. *Pinocchio in Emojitaliano*. Sesto Fiorentino: Apice libri.

Herbert H Clark. 2003. Pointing and placing. In *Pointing: Where language, culture, and cognition meet*, volume 243, page 268.

Greville G Corbett. 2000. *Number*. Cambridge University Press.

William Croft, D Alan Cruse, et al. 2004. *Cognitive linguistics*. Cambridge University Press.

Philippe Dessus and Daniel Peraya. 2005. Le rôle des connaissances dans l'identification automatique d'icones. *Revue des Sciences et Technologies de l'Information-Série RIA: Revue d'Intelligence Artificielle*, 19:195–214.

Jennifer Ferreira, Pippin Barr, and James Noble. 2005. The semiotics of user interface redesign. In *Proceedings of the Sixth Australasian conference on User interface-Volume 40*, pages 47–53.

Charles J Fillmore and Collin Baker. 2010. A frames approach to semantic analysis. In *The Oxford handbook of linguistic analysis*.

Lauren Gawne and Jennifer Daniel. 2021. The past and future of hand emoji. In *Proceedings of the 4th International Workshop on Emoji Understanding and Applications in Social Media*.

Jing Ge and Susan C Herring. 2018. Communicative functions of emoji sequences on sina weibo. *First Monday*.

Regina Gutiérrez Pérez. 2008. A cross-cultural analysis of heart metaphors.

Elisabetta Ježek. 2016. *The lexicon: An introduction*. Oxford university press.

Adam Kilgarriff, Vít Baisa, Jan Bušta, Miloš Jakubíček, Vojtěch Kovář, Jan Michelfeit, Pavel Rychlỳ, and Vít Suchomel. 2014. The sketch engine: ten years on. *Lexicography*, 1(1):7–36.

Artie Konrad, Susan C Herring, and David Choi. 2020. Sticker and emoji use in facebook messenger: Implications for graphicon change. *Journal of Computer-Mediated Communication*, 25(3):217–235.

Yohei Kurata and Max J Egenhofer. 2005. Semantics of simple arrow diagrams. In *AAAI Spring Symposium: Reasoning with Mental and External Diagrams: Computational Modeling and Spatial Assistance*, pages 101–104.

Dieudonné Leclercq. 1992. *Audio-visuel et apprentissage*. Université de Liège - Service de Technologie de l'Education, Liège.

David Matsumoto and Hyisung C Hwang. 2013. Cultural similarities and differences in emblematic gestures. *Journal of Nonverbal Behavior*, 37(1):1–27.

George A Miller. 1998. *WordNet: An electronic lexical database*. MIT press.

Claudio Nobili. 2018. Francesca chiusaroli, johanna monti, federico sangati, pinocchio in emojitaliano. apice libri, sesto fiorentino (fi), 2017. *Lingue e culture dei media*, 2(1):173–176.

Nuno Emanuel Branquinho Moutinho Marques de Paiva. 2018. *Using emoji in an e-commerce context: effects in brand perception, quality of service and intention to recommend*. Ph.D. thesis.

Rupal Patel, Sam Pilato, and Deb Roy. 2004. Beyond linear syntax: An image-oriented communication aid. *Assistive Technology Outcomes and Benefits*, 1(1):57–66.

Eva Eriva Tandi Payuk and Zakrimal Zakrimal. 2020. Semiotic analysis in instagram logo. *IDEAS: Journal on English Language Teaching and Learning, Linguistics and Literature*, 8(1):332–339.

Daniel Peraya, Didier Strasser, et al. 1999. L'iconomètre: un outil de formation et de recherche pour mesurer le degré de polysémie des représentations visuelles. In *Université ouverte, formation virtuelle et apprentissage (Communications francophones du cinquième Colloque européen sur l'autoformation, Barcelone*, pages 225–236.

Cesco Reale, Marwan Kilani, Araceli Giménez, Nadu Barbashova, and Roman Oechslin. 2021. From hieroglyphs to emoji, to ikon: The search of the (perfect?) visual language. In *International Conference on Human-Computer Interaction*, pages 457–476. Springer.

Eleanor Rosch, Carolyn B Mervis, Wayne D Gray, David M Johnson, and Penny Boyes-Braem. 1976. Basic objects in natural categories. *Cognitive psychology*, 8(3):382–439.

Carol Tenny. 2016. A linguist looks at aac: Language representation systems for augmentative and alternative communication, compared with writing systems and natural language. *Writing Systems Research*, 8(1):84–119.

Charles Tijus, Javier Barcenilla, Brigitte Cambon De Lavalette, and Jean-Guy Meunier. 2007. The design, understanding and usage of pictograms. In *Written documents in the workplace*, pages 17–31. Brill.

David P Wilkins and Deborah Hill. 1995. When go means come: Questioning the basicness of basic motion verbs.

Ning Yu. 2000. Figurative uses of finger and palm in chinese and english. *Metaphor and symbol*, 15(3):159–175.

Emoji semantics/pragmatics: investigating commitment and lying

Benjamin Weissman
Rensselaer Polytechnic Institute – Department of Cognitive Science
weissb2@rpi.edu

Abstract

This paper presents the results of two experiments investigating the directness of emoji in constituting speaker meaning. This relationship is examined in two ways, with Experiment 1 testing whether speakers are committed to meanings they communicate via a single emoji and Experiment 2 testing whether that speaker is taken to have lied if that meaning is false and intended to deceive. Results indicate that emoji with high meaning agreement in general (i.e., pictorial representations of concrete objects or foods) reliably commit the speaker to that meaning and can constitute lying. Expressive emoji representing facial expressions and emotional states demonstrate a range of commitment and lie ratings: those with high meaning agreement constitute more commitment and more of a lie than those with less meaning agreement in the first place. Emoji can constitute speaker commitment and they can be lies, but this result does not apply uniformly to all emoji and is instead tied to agreement, conventionality, and lexicalization.

1 Introduction

Despite a multitude of studies focusing on emoji meanings, there has not yet been much research on the nature of these meanings with respect to semantics and pragmatics. The present research steps in this direction by investigating the relationships between emoji meaning and commitment and emoji meaning and lying. This paper presents the results of two studies probing the extent to which emoji constitute speaker commitment to content and the possibility of lying via emoji in order to better understand perceptions of the strength of meaning of emoji.

Studies on emoji meaning have ranged from how emoji supplement text with pragmatic information like irony (Garcia et al., 2022; Weissman & Tanner, 2018), emotional valence (Pfeifer et al., 2022), and indirect meaning (Holtgraves & Robinson, 2020) to more direct investigations of emoji meaning ratings and norms (Rodrigues et al., 2018; Was & Hamrick, 2021). In light of the wide range of communicative functions that emoji can fulfill (e.g., Beißwenger & Pappert, 2019; Dainas & Herring, 2021; Ge & Herring, 2018; Logi & Zappavigna, 2021; Yang & Liu, 2021), the nature of emoji meanings across these varied uses is rich ground for further research.

In research at the semantics/pragmatics interface, commitment offers a way to explore the meaning-making process – what we take a speaker to mean is related to what we take that speaker to having committed to. This has recently been explored with respect to inferences, such as presuppositions, implicatures, and explicatures. The link established from this research thus far ties together the notions of commitment, expression directness, and meaning: a more direct expression yields greater commitment and stronger meaning (e.g., Bonalumi et al., 2020; Boulat & Maillat, 2017; Mazzarella et al., 2018; Moeschler, 2013; Vullioud et al., 2017). An implicature, for example, communicates content less directly than saying that content literally; the speaker is thus less committed to the implicated content than the directly-said content. There is no universal definition for commitment, but it can be explored by testing whether speakers are taken as committed to certain propositions. Another lens with which to view this is deniability (e.g., Boogaart et al., 2021): an indirect (i.e., implicated) expression of content theoretically leaves the speaker room to deny that what the hearer understood is not what they

Proceedings of the The Fifth International Workshop on Emoji Understanding and Applications in Social Media, pages 21 - 28
July 14, 2022 ©2022 Association for Computational Linguistics

intended to mean with their utterance, while a direct expression of that content leaves the speaker no such room.

A recent proposal claims that an utterance can only be a lie if the speaker is committed to the relevant content (Reins & Wiegmann, 2021). If a speaker implies something false, but is not committed to that implicated content, the speaker is not taken to have lied. This is consistent with theoretical proposals (e.g., Saul, 2012) and experimental evidence (Weissman & Terkourafi, 2019) claiming that delivering false content through implicature is "merely misleading" rather than outright lying. Recent approaches have also provided support for the idea of lying in different modalities, like Viebahn's (2019) investigation of lying with pictures – the present study tests extending this claim to emoji, a conventionalized and (to varying extents) lexicalized set of pictures.

The present research weaves together these threads of research to assess the link between emoji and speaker meaning via commitment and lying – are speakers committed to what they "say" if what they "say" is an emoji? Is it possible to lie via emoji? As emoji continue to grow in popularity (and, correspondingly, conventionality), perceptions of emoji constituting commitment and lying may change over time as well, consistent with the finding that emoji meaning changes over time (Robertson et al., 2021).

An important nuance to acknowledge in an emoji investigation like this is that not all emoji are the same; we should not necessarily expect all emoji to constitute speaker commitment in the same way. At the very least, there appear to be two broad categories of emoji: those that realistically depict real-world objects, animals, foods, etc. and those that more symbolically represent concepts like facial expressions, gestures, and other expressive meanings (see Grosz et al. (2021) for a semantic analysis demonstrating group differences between what they call "face" emoji and "activity" emoji or Maier (2021) for a different analysis between "entity" emoji and "facial expression" emoji). Just as there are different implicature types that do not all contribute to meaning in exactly the same way with exactly the same strength (e.g. Ariel, 2019; Doran et al., 2012; van Tiel et al., 2016), we may, too, expect similar nuance in emoji meaning-making.

Another level of nuance comes from emoji meaning agreement – not all emoji are equally unambiguous in their links to meaning. 🍓 seems fairly clear and unambiguous in its representation of a strawberry, but an emoji like 😒 may mean different things to different people and in different contexts. To get an appropriately nuanced picture of the link between emoji and meaning, these experiments will test two sets of emoji: one set of high-meaning-agreement non-expressive emoji (objects, foods, and animals) and another set of expressive emoji (facial expressions and bodily gestures) that demonstrate a wide range of meaning agreement.

This paper presents the results of two experiments aimed at assessing the relationship between emoji and meaning commitment. The first experiment asks directly about commitment and deniability (partially following the approach used by Reins & Wiegmann (2021)); the second experiment probes lie ratings.

If emoji are found to yield uniformly less commitment and lower lie ratings than words, that would suggest that emoji are less direct in their meaning than words and as such contribute less strongly to speaker meaning. If emoji are found to yield uniformly as much commitment as words (with equal lie ratings), that would suggest that emoji are as direct in their meaning as words. A third possibility is that different emoji yield a range of attributions of commitment and lie ratings, which would suggest that emoji are capable of delivering speaker meaning but not all emoji do so in exactly the same way – we would thus end up with a more nuanced account of how emoji contribute to meaning, potentially related to emoji meaning agreement and consistency.

2 Pretest

Two meaning agreement surveys were carried out to hone in on the set of emoji to be used in the experiments, one for the non-expressive group and one for the expressive group. In both cases, participants were presented with a list of emoji and instructed to type in the meaning for each. Results were manually categorized by two raters into bins for each emoji and these bins were then ordered according to frequency. These results thus yield an agreement proportion for every emoji tested; if 92% of participants write that 🍅 means "tomato," that emoji has an agreement of 0.92. Synonyms (e.g., "happy" and "glad") were binned together but similar non-synonyms (e.g., "happy" and "smiling") were binned separately.

Data for the non-expressive group was collected on 80 emoji from 49 participants (average age = 30.29 (sd = 13.5), 41 female, 8 male) as part of another experiment; participants were compensated with course credit. was chosen manually. The 80 emoji chosen included foods, objects, and animals that were expected to have reasonably high agreement across participants. A set of 20 emoji all with agreement over 0.75 (average agreement = 0.88 (sd = 0.05)) were selected for use in the experiment.

Data for the expressive group was collected from a new set of 28 participants (average age = 31 (sd = 11.6), 22 female, 6 male). These participants were compensated $2.55 USD for their participation in the survey, for an average prorated compensation of $12.90/hr. 75 emoji, primarily gesture and facial expression emoji, were tested; from this group, a set of 20 emoji were selected for use in the experiment (average agreement = 0.62 (sd = 0.23)). Importantly, this set covered a range of agreement from 0.25 to 0.96.

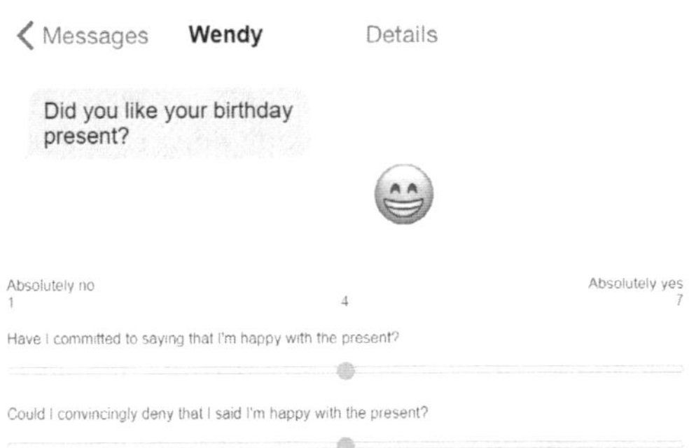

Figure 1 - Example stimulus from Experiment 1.

3 Experiment 1

Experiment 1 investigated the extent to which emoji messages yield commitment and deniability.

3.1 Methods

The emoji selected from the pretests were turned into experimental stimuli by creating question-answer pairs where the answer is a single emoji. These are presented as text messages that I (the experimenter) have received and sent. For each item, participants were asked to provide two ratings, corresponding to direct commitment ("Have I committed to saying X?" and deniability ("Could I convincingly deny that I said X?"). Ratings were provided on a sliding scale. An example is provided below in Figure 1.

100 participants (average age = 32.4; 72 female, 25 male, 2 non-binary, 1 not reported) recruited from Prolific participated in Experiment 1. Participants were compensated $2.00 USD for their participation in the short survey, for an average prorated compensation of around $18/hr.

Each participant saw 20 items. For 10 of these, the question matched the most-commonly-provided meaning for the emoji; for 10 of these, the question asked about some other meaning that was clearly not present in the text message. These mismatch trials should, in theory, always receive a score at the low end of the scale – it would be rare for a participant to interpret 😑 as "excited" or 🐘 as "elephant." The mismatching set was included as fillers to counterbalance the experimental items, and the specific ratings given for any item in that condition are dependent upon the exact mismatching alternative provided; as such, these are not discussed further in analysis here. So that every emoji could be seen equally in both conditions, 4 lists were created. Each participant saw 10 expressive emoji items and 10 non-expressive emoji items, counterbalanced across the match/mismatch conditions.

3.2 Results

Results given on the sliding scale were converted to a traditional 1-7 scale. The direct commitment and (inversed) deniability ratings were merged into a single commitment rating for each participant for item. Overall, as shown in Figure 2, the non-expressive set (average = 6.09, sd = 1.11) yielded significantly higher commitment ratings than the expressive set (5.17, sd = 1.59) as modeled by a linear mixed effects model with random slopes for emoji type and random intercepts for participant ($F(1,99) = 114.2$, $p < .001$).

The expressive set was investigated further to clarify the relationship between agreement and commitment. There was a significant effect of pre-test agreement ratings on commitment ratings according to the linear mixed effects model with random slopes for emoji type and random intercepts for participant ($F(1,998) = 20.5$, $p < .001$). Emoji that demonstrated lower population-wide agreement yielded lower commitment ratings in this task; emoji with higher agreement yielded higher commitment ratings. This correlative relationship is shown in Figure 3.

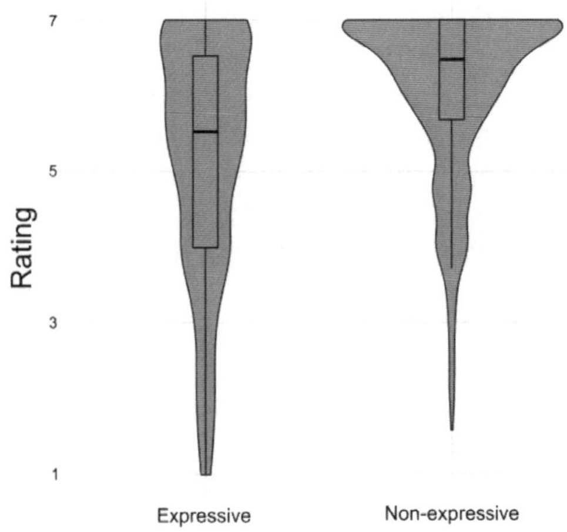

Figure 3 - Violin plot of commitment/deniability ratings for expressive and non-expressive emoji in Experiment 1. Horizontal bar in each column represents median; boxes extend to first and third quartiles.

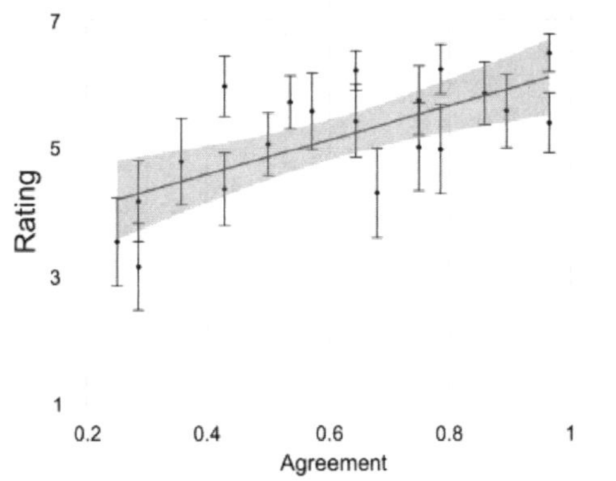

Figure 4 - Correlative relationship between pretest emoji meaning agreement and Experiment 1 commitment/deniability ratings.

4 Experiment 2

Experiment 2 investigates the extent to which it is possible to lie via emoji.

4.1 Methods

The same question/answer text messages from Experiment 1 were used in Experiment 2 with context added. The context was in the form of a few sentences presented above the text message picture and worked to establish whether the answer that I provide in the text message is true or false. In the true condition, the context reveals that my answer is true (i.e., matches what really happened or what I really believe to be true); in the false condition, the context revealed that my answer is false (i.e., does not match what happened or what I believe to be true) and includes motivation for me to deceive the interlocutor. An example of the "lie" condition

Figure 2 - Example stimulus from Experiment 2.

is shown in Figure 4.

202 new participants (average age = 33.7, sd = 10.3; 151 female, 50 male, 1 genderqueer), none of whom participated in Experiment 1, were recruited from Prolific. Data from 7 participants was discarded due to consistently unreliable answers to filler items, yielding a final dataset from 195 participants.

As in Experiment 1, 4 lists were created, each with 10 expressive and 10 non-expressive emoji, counterbalanced across 10 true and 10 false responses. In this experiment, however, those 4 lists were repeated with word responses instead of emoji responses to allow for a word vs. emoji comparison.

4.2 Results

A linear mixed effects model with random intercepts for participant estimated a significant interaction between type (expressive/non-expressive) and presentation (word/emoji) ($F(1,1753) = 3.90$, $p = 0.48$). Lie ratings for emoji were significantly lower than lie ratings for words, but this difference was significantly greater for expressive items than non-expressive items. Figure 5 portrays this relationship graphically.

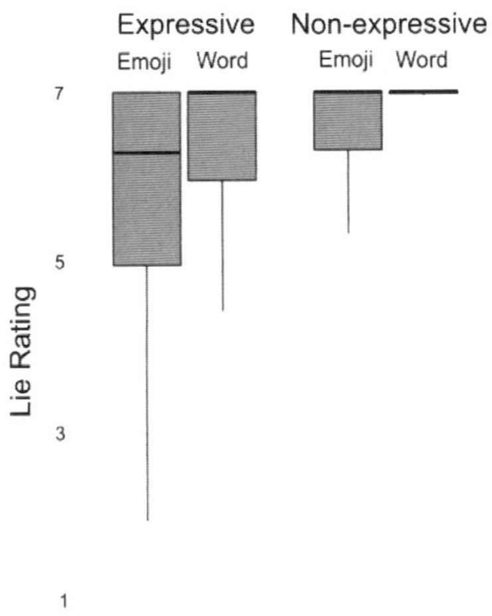

Figure 5 - Boxplot depicting lie ratings for expressive and non-expressive emoji and words. Horizontal line in each column represents median; boxes extend to first and third quartiles.

The expressive set was again investigated further to explore the relationship between commitment and lie ratings for emoji messages. A linear mixed effects model with random intercepts for participant yielded a significant effect of commitment on lie ratings ($F(1,432) = 15.13$, $p < .001$) in the expected direction – emoji to which participants in Experiment 1 attributed a higher degree of commitment yielded higher lie ratings in Experiment 2 when the message meaning is revealed to be false.

5 Discussion

These two experiments have provided evidence that emoji can constitute speaker commitment and it is possible to lie via emoji, but the extent to which they contribute to speaker meaning is not the same for all emoji. Emoji that have high meaning agreement in the first place (from another perspective, emoji that are farther along in the lexicalization or conventionalization process) contribute more directly to speaker meaning; the correlative relationships between agreement, commitment, and lie ratings highlight this finding. A fully lexicalized emoji with high meaning agreement and consistency does not leave much room for varying interpretation and accordingly yield the speaker less deniability. Though the focus of this paper is on emoji themselves, further study in this direction can work towards establishing a taxonomy of semantic/pragmatic commitment across modalities.

In these results, there is a distinction between expressive emoji (e.g., facial expressions) and non-expressive emoji (e.g., objects) with respect to commitment and lying, but this is mediated by their meaning agreement in the first place. In other words, non-expressive emoji do not inherently contribute more to commitment than expressive emoji, but this difference surfaces because non-expressive emoji are more likely to be direct and unambiguous representations of their assigned meanings. On the other hand, expressive emoji are likely to contain more ambiguity and potential polysemy, yielding less agreement over their meanings in the first place. This finding is highlighted by the significant correlation between agreement and commitment among the expressive emoji tested.

Further research can explore the context-sensitivity of these relationships. Since context significantly affects both lie ratings (Weissman, 2019a) and emoji interpretations (e.g., Miller et al., 2017; Weissman, 2019b), a more nuanced look at this complex relationship is likely warranted. As recent work has begun exploring multi-emoji sequences and the extent to which those are (un)natural forms of expressing content (e.g., Cohn et al., 2019; Herring & Ge, 2020; McCulloch & Gawne, 2018), this endeavor could benefit from a commitment-based analysis as well. Discussions of emoji interpretation challenges in the courtroom has already begun (e.g., Foltz & Fray, 2020). In today's age, it does not seem far-fetched to imagine a public figure mired in an emoji-related scandal – such an occasion would certainly provide a fascinating case study for the deniability and commitment of emoji.

Acknowledgments

Thank you to Camdyn Vanek for their assistance in developing materials to be used in this research.

References

Ariel, M. (2019). Different prominences for different inferences. Journal of Pragmatics, 154, 103–116.

Beißwenger, M., & Pappert, S. (2019). How to be polite with emoji: A pragmatic analysis of face work strategies in an online learning environment. European Journal of Applied Linguistics, 7(2), 225–253.

Bonalumi, F., Scott-Phillips, T., Tacha, J., & Heintz, C. (2020). Commitment and communication: Are we committed to what we mean, or what we say? Language and Cognition, 12(2), 360–384.

Boogaart, R., Jansen, H., & van Leeuwen, M. (2021). "Those are your words, not mine!" Defence strategies for denying speaker commitment. Argumentation, 35(2), 209–235.

Boulat, K., & Maillat, D. (2017). She said you said I saw it with my own eyes: a pragmatic account of commitment. In Formal models in the study of language (pp. 261–279). Springer.

Cohn, N., Engelen, J., & Schilperoord, J. (2019). The grammar of emoji? Constraints on communicative pictorial sequencing. Cognitive Research: Principles and Implications, 4(1).

Dainas, A. R., & Herring, S. C. (2021). Interpreting emoji pragmatics. Approaches to Internet Pragmatics, 107-144.

Doran, R., Ward, G., Larson, M., McNabb, Y., & Baker, R. E. (2012). A novel experimental paradigm for distinguishing between what is said and what is implicated. Language, 88(1), 124–154.

Foltz, K. A., & Fray, J. (2020). Emoji goes to court: An analysis of emoji in court proceedings and implications for legal practice. Communication Law Review, 20, 109-125.

Garcia, C., Ţurcan, A., Howman, H., & Filik, R. (2022). Emoji as a tool to aid the comprehension of written sarcasm: Evidence from younger and older adults. Computers in Human Behavior, 126(August 2021), 106971.

Ge, J., & Herring, S. C. (2018). Communicative functions of emoji sequences on Sina Weibo. First Monday, 23(11).

Grosz, P., Kaiser, E., & Pierini, F. (2021). Discourse anaphoricity and first-person indexicality in emoji resolution. Proceedings of Sinn Und Bedeutung, 25.

Herring, S., & Ge, J. (2020). Do Emoji Sequences Have a Preferred Word Order? 14th International AAAI Conference on Web and Social Media, (June), 1–5.

Holtgraves, T., & Robinson, C. (2020). Emoji can facilitate recognition of conveyed indirect meaning. PLoS ONE, 15(4), 1–13.

Logi, L., & Zappavigna, M. (2021). A social semiotic perspective on emoji: How emoji and language interact to make meaning in digital messages. New Media and Society, (September).

Maier, E. (2021). Emoji as pictures. Under review. https://ling.auf.net/lingbuzz/006025.

Mazzarella, D., Reinecke, R., Noveck, I., & Mercier, H. (2018). Saying, presupposing and implicating: How pragmatics modulates commitment. Journal of Pragmatics, 133(June), 15–27.

McCulloch, G., & Gawne, L. (2018). Emoji grammar as beat gestures. CEUR Workshop Proceedings, 2130, 3–6.

Miller, H., Kluver, D., Thebault-Spieker, J., Terveen, L., & Hecht, B. (2017). Understanding Emoji Ambiguity in Context: The Role of Text in Emoji-Related Miscommunication. Proceedings of the Eleventh International AAAI Conference on Web and Social Media, 152–161.

Moeschler, J. (2013). Is a speaker-based pragmatics possible? Or how can a hearer infer a speaker's commitment? Journal of Pragmatics, 48(1), 84–97.

Pfeifer, V. A., Armstrong, E. L., & Lai, V. T. (2022). Do all facial emoji communicate emotion? The impact of facial emoji on perceived sender emotion and text processing. Computers in Human Behavior, 126, 107016.

Reins, L. M., & Wiegmann, A. (2021). Is lying bound to commitment? Empirically investigating deceptive presuppositions, implicatures, and actions. Cognitive Science, 45(2).

Robertson, A., Liza, F. F., Nguyen, D., McGillivray, B., & Hale, S. A. (2021). Semantic journeys: quantifying change in emoji meaning from 2012-2018. Emoji2021. http://workshop-proceedings.icwsm.org/pdf/2021_07.pdf

Rodrigues, D., Prada, M., Gaspar, R., Garrido, M. V., & Lopes, D. (2018). Lisbon Emoji and Emoticon Database (LEED): Norms for emoji and emoticons in seven evaluative dimensions. Behavior Research Methods, 50(1), 392–405.

Saul, J. M. (2012). Lying, Misleading, and What is Said: An Exploration in Philosophy of Language and in Ethics. Oxford: Oxford University Press.

van Tiel, B., van Miltenburg, E., Zevakhina, N., & Geurts, B. (2016). Scalar diversity. Journal of Semantics, 33(1), 137–175.

Viebahn, E. (2019). Lying with pictures. British Journal of Aesthetics, 59(3), 243–257.

Vullioud, C., Clément, F., Scott-Phillips, T., & Mercier, H. (2017). Confidence as an expression of commitment: why misplaced expressions of confidence backfire. Evolution and Human Behavior, 38(1), 9–17.

Was, C. A., & Hamrick, P. (2021). What Did They Mean by That? Young Adults' Interpretations of 105 Common Emoji. Frontiers in Psychology, 12(May), 1–7.

Weissman, B. (2019a). The role of linguistic meaning in the concept of lying. PhD Dissertation. University of Illinois at Urbana-Champaign.

Weissman, B. (2019b). Peaches and eggplants or. . . something else? The role of context in emoji interpretations. Proceedings of the Linguistic Society of America, 4(1), 29.

Weissman, B., & Tanner, D. (2018). A strong wink between verbal and emoji-based irony: How the brain processes ironic emoji during language comprehension. PLoS ONE, 13(8).

Weissman, B., & Terkourafi, M. (2019). Are false implicatures lies? An experimental investigation. Mind & Language, 34(2), 221–246.

Yang, X., & Liu, M. (2021). The pragmatics of text-emoji co-occurrences on Chinese social media. Pragmatics, 31(1), 144–172.

A Supplementary Material

Materials and data are available at: https://osf.io/wtnzy/?view_only=48586c4d47f946fd9efc1044c995e32e

B Appendix

This appendix lists the emoji used in the experiment, the most-commonly-provided meaning for each emoji from the pre-test, and the agreement rating for each emoji from the pre-test. Expressive emoji appear in Table 1; non-expressive in Table 2.

Emoji	Meaning	Agreement
😠	angry	.964
🤪	silly	.964
😎	cool	.893
😮	shocked	.857
🥳	celebrate	.786
🤐	lips are sealed	.786
😘	kiss	.750
😇	angel	.750
😐	neutral	.679
😁	happy	.643
😭	crying	.643
😫	upset	.571
🥱	tired	.536
😨	afraid	.500
😰	stressed	.429
😶	no words	.429
😬	cringe	.358
😑	annoyed	.286
💁‍♀️	sassy	.286
🥴	goofy	.250

Table 1: expressive emoji used in both experiments

Emoji	Meaning	Agreement
⛪	church	0.959
🏥	hospital	0.959
🍅	tomato	0.939
🕷	spider	0.918
🔑	key	0.918
🏰	castle	0.918
🍩	donut	0.918
🥗	salad	0.898
🚲	bike	0.898
🏀	basketball	0.898
🧑‍🚀	astronaut	0.878
🥞	pancakes	0.878
🌮	taco	0.878
🍇	grapes	0.878
🐍	snake	0.857
🐉	dragon	0.857
🎢	roller coaster	0.837
🎻	violin	0.816
🏈	football	0.776
📎	paper clip	0.776

Table 2: non-expressive emoji used in both experiments

Understanding the Sarcastic Nature of Emojis with SarcOji

Vandita Grover
Research Scholar
Department of Computer Science
University of Delhi
vgrover@cs.du.ac.in

Hema Banati
Professor
Dyal Singh College
Lodhi Road, University of Delhi
hemabanati@dsc.du.ac.in

Abstract

Identifying sarcasm is a challenging research problem owing to its highly contextual nature. Several researchers have attempted numerous mechanisms to incorporate context, linguistic aspects, and supervised and semi-supervised techniques to determine sarcasm. It has also been noted that emojis in a text may also hold key indicators of sarcasm. However, the availability of sarcasm datasets with emojis is scarce. This makes it challenging to effectively study the sarcastic nature of emojis. In this work, we present SarcOji which has been compiled from five publicly available sarcasm datasets. SarcOji contains labeled English texts which all have emojis. We also analyze SarcOji to determine if there is an incongruence in the polarity of text and emojis used therein. Further, emojis' usage, occurrences, and positions in the context of sarcasm are also studied in this compiled dataset. With SarcOji we have been able to demonstrate that frequency of occurrence of an emoji and its position are strong indicators of sarcasm. SarcOji dataset is now publicly available with several derived features like sentiment scores of text and emojis, most frequent emoji, and its position in the text. Compilation of the SarcOji dataset is an initial step to enable the study of the role of emojis in communicating sarcasm. SarcOji dataset can also serve as a go-to dataset for various emoji-based sarcasm detection techniques.

1 Introduction

Sarcasm detection has piqued significant interest in various research communities, be it linguistics, psychology, or computational. Identifying sarcasm requires context and background which become a challenge for computational models (Ghosh et al., 2017). Joshi et al. (2017) identify three approaches to sarcasm detection, viz., rule-based, statistical (feature and learning-based), and deep-learning approaches. They also identify issues with these approaches. For instance, if we deal with the sentiment (read polarity) as a feature, it may mislead a classifier because the surface sentiment might be different from the intent. They also note that in general sarcasm datasets are skewed in favor of non-sarcastic sentences.

Joshi et al. (2015) talk about *Explicit Incongruity* where words of both positive and negative polarities are present in a sarcastic text. While *Implicit Incongruity* may be expressed through an implied sentiment. Many researchers have incorporated context and exploited context incongruity for sarcasm detection tasks (Joshi et al., 2015), (Ghosh et al., 2017), (Ghosh and Veale, 2017), (Joshi et al., 2018), (Hazarika et al., 2018), (Jena et al., 2020). But we opine that context may not always be available in real-world scenarios. For instance, in (Razali et al., 2017) it is noted that apart from text and context outside the target, other modalities, too, are important for sarcasm detection; especially when the research trend is to use deep learning networks in sarcasm detection tasks. Such classifiers need features that can be extracted by exploring other modalities. Grover (2021) discussed how interest in learning emoji embeddings and using emojis for sentiment classification has evolved in the past few years. This work also discussed the need to explore the role of emojis to uncover complex and nuanced expressions of sarcasm and irony. On the other hand, many works have attempted to incorporate mixed or opposite polarities in sentences to detect sarcasm, (J and Ravikumar, 2019), (Tewani, 2019). Apart from lexical features, researchers are also attempting to explore other features like slang, emoticons, emojis, reviews, etc. for sarcasm detection (Sundararajan et al., 2021). In this work we focus on emojis to understand if and how they contribute to expressing sarcasm. We set to answer the following questions.

1. Is there any incongruence between the polarity of emojis and that of text they occur with?

Proceedings of the The Fifth International Workshop on Emoji Understanding and Applications in Social Media, pages 29 - 39
July 14, 2022 ©2022 Association for Computational Linguistics

2. Are there any specific emojis that users tend to use with sarcastic texts?

3. Is there a relationship between the intensity (frequency) of emojis used in the text and underlying sarcasm?

4. Is there a relationship between the position of occurrence of an emoji and the sarcastic nature of the text?

Therefore we compile from various benchmark and emoji datasets to create a labeled Sarcasm Dataset - SarcOji. SarcOji has text records, all with emojis. These records are augmented with derived features like sentiment scores of text and emojis. Sentiment analysis tools like SentiWordNet (Esuli and Sebastiani, 2006), (Baccianella et al., 2010), VADER (Hutto and Gilbert, 2014), TextBlob [1], and Emoji Sentiment Ranking (Kralj Novak et al., 2015) are used to compute sentiment scores. We compute sentiment scores to extract text and emoji polarities. Moreover, these numerical features may be useful in training machine or deep learning classifiers for sarcasm detection. We also capture the most frequent emoji in the text along with its frequency and position of occurrence for an in-depth analysis of emoji usage in sarcastic texts.
The rest of the paper is organized into four sections. In Related Work, various experiments and studies on emojis and sarcasm are discussed. In the Methodology section, we elaborate on the compilation of the SarcOji dataset from five publicly available sarcasm datasets. We also discuss our mechanism to determine incongruence between the sentiment of text and emojis and determine the position of the most frequent emoji in the text. In the subsequent section, we report our observations and inferences from the SarcOji dataset. In the last section, we conclude and identify directions for future work in utilizing emojis for sarcasm detection.

2 Related Work

Emojis are now one of the preferred modalities in sentiment analysis tasks. There have been many resources that are publicly available for use to identify emoji sentiments and the sense in which emojis are used. But, these resources do not holistically capture the sarcastic nature of emojis. The Emoji Sentiment Ranking (ESR) by Kralj Novak et al. (2015) computes the sentiment of 751 popular emojis from the sentiment of the tweets where these emojis are used. In this work, it is also reported that the emojis with high sentiment scores (negative or positive) occur towards the end of the tweet and on average, an emoji occurs at a two-thirds length of a tweet. But ESR does not capture the sentiment of the latest emojis which makes it difficult to fully utilize its strengths.
A machine-readable emoji inventory linking emoji Unicode representations with their English meanings is presented in EmojiNet (Wijeratne et al., 2017a). This inventory contains different senses (noun, verb, adjective), etc. in which an emoji can be used. EmojiNet can be used in the disambiguation of emoji senses and identifying similarities between emojis. While this is a very powerful resource for emoji disambiguation, how these senses can be used to determine sarcasm is yet to be explored.
Wijeratne et al. (2017b) compiled the EmoSim508 dataset with similarity scores of 508 pairs of emojis. In this work, EmojiNet was used to extract word descriptions of emojis and learn emoji embeddings. Several experiments have been carried out to observe emoji usage across social media and how can they be used to capture sarcasm.
Zhao et al. (2018) analyzed emoji usage on social media and observed that 70% of emojis occurred towards the end of the tweets, while only 2.6% are used at the beginning. Thompson et al. (2016) conducted experiments with 51 participants and found that emoticons were used more in sarcastic texts. They also reported that tongue and wink face are strong indicators of sarcasm. Garcia et al. (2022) report that emojis can help both young and older adults discern sarcasm. Miller et al. (2017) refute the previous hypothesis that emojis when placed with textual context may reduce miscommunication. They concur that surrounding text does not reduce emoji ambiguity and attribute this result to possible sarcasm.
Many researchers have conducted experiments to incorporate emojis in sarcasm classification tasks. Felbo et al. (2017) built a large text corpus with emojis to learn emotional content, sarcasm, and sentiment detection in texts. They created a pretrained model called DeepMoji. But the success of DeepMoji heavily relied on tweets and their length. Wang et al. (2021) used the speaker's prior probability of sarcasm and embedded emojis to recognize

[1] https://buildmedia.readthedocs.org/media/pdf/textblob/latest/textblob.pdf

sarcasm. Rustagi et al. (2022) integrate emojis, ratings, and reviews to enhance sarcasm classification tasks. Tewani (2019) uses polarity of texts, emojis, and hashtags to classify sarcasm on a small dataset of 650 tweets.

There have been different approaches to understanding emoji usage, emoji sense, and incorporating emojis to detect sarcasm, but we are yet to come across a study that attempts to investigate whether popular emojis used with sarcasm or if they are indeed incongruent with the surrounding text or does their position or frequency matter when sarcasm is expressed?

We now move ahead to describe the compilation and analysis of a dedicated sarcasm dataset with emojis - SarcOji.

3 Methodology

In this section, we describe the various sources from which the SarcOji dataset was compiled. We further list down steps to mine frequent emojis used in the dataset and how sentiment scores of the text, as well as emojis, were computed using different tools.

3.1 Data Collection

For compiling SarcOji datasets 5 publicly available Sarcasm datasets were utilized, viz.

1. Sarcasm Dataset harvested from Twitter by Ghosh and Veale (2016).

2. Dataset compiled by Subramanian et al. (2019) to detect sarcasm using emojis. The dataset is compiled from Twitter and Facebook posts.

3. Oprea and Magdy (2019) curated a Dataset for intended sarcasm by asking Twitter users to provide links to their sarcastic (1) and non-sarcastic (3) tweets. For the sarcastic tweet user also provided information on why it was sarcastic and a non-sarcastic rephrase of the same message.

4. Shared Task on Sarcasm (Twitter and Reddit) dataset at FigLang'2020 (Ghosh et al., 2020). This dataset has been compiled from the self-annotated Reddit corpus of sarcastic texts by Khodak et al. (2017).

5. Intended Sarcasm Dataset in English from iSarcasmEval Task at SemEval'22 Abu Farha et al. (2022). The sarcastic labels of the texts are provided by the text authors. Each sarcastic text is also rephrased by the text author to convey the intended message without sarcasm. The sarcastic texts are additionally labeled by linguists into one of the ironic speech categories like irony, satire, overstatement, understatement, rhetorical question, etc. (Gibbs Jr et al., 2002)

Dataset	Sarcastic	Non-Sarcastic
(Ghosh and Veale, 2016)	18000	21000
(Subramanian et al., 2019)	9260	13070
(Oprea and Magdy, 2019)	2500	2500
(Ghosh et al., 2020)	777	3707
(Abu Farha et al., 2022)	867	2601
(iSarcasmEval SubTask)		
Total	31404	42872

Table 1: Source Datasets' Statistics

These datasets were used as Ghosh and Veale (2016) , Oprea and Magdy (2019), Ghosh et al. (2020) along with the recent SemEval-2022 Abu Farha et al. (2022) are publicly available benchmark datasets, while Subramanian et al. (2019) is another popular dataset that contains a large number of texts with emojis. Moreover, after combining these datasets we have heterogeneity of sources (Twitter and Facebook) from which data is collected.

To gather as many records as possible we combined records from the train and test sets of the above mentioned datasets. The source datasets' statistics are given in Table 1.

3.2 Data Preprocessing

Before mining this dataset a few preprocessing steps were undertaken, as listed below:

1. Renaming the attributes(column) as Text for text/tweet column and Sarcastic to determine if the Text is sarcastic or not. Since all the datasets came from different sources so their column names, order, and the number of columns differed. We retained only the Text/Tweets and the column specifying their sarcastic nature. Columns like rephrase of sarcastic text, type of sarcasm, etc. were dropped for preparation of SarcOji as we wanted to only focus on how emojis were used with sarcastic texts.

2. The Sarcastic Column was label-encoded to 0,1 for uniformity. The source datasets had

different ways to represent sarcasm, for instance, Sarcastic, Not_Sarcastic, SARCASM, NON_SARCASM. Thus, all the sarcastic texts were label-encoded as 1, and 0 otherwise.

3. All the records where the language source was not English were dropped using the Google Trans API [2]. For example, if the text was "Bonjour", then it was dropped. This was done to ensure that the sentiment scores were computed correctly.

4. The text was also cleaned to remove URLs (HTTP(s), mentions(@), and hashtags (#).

5. The texts that did not contain any emojis were dropped too.

After preprocessing the combined dataset had 29377 labeled records with 11448 sarcastic and 17929 non-sarcastic texts with emojis.

3.3 Mining Frequent Emojis

The next step was to mine the frequent emojis used in the dataset. For every text, the most frequent emoji was found and the emoji and its number of occurrences in the text in consideration were also stored. We also computed the position of the first occurrence of the most frequent emoji in a text. This task can be done using a linear scan of the text and applying regular expressions for Unicode emojis or *advertools* package [3] can also be used. Some examples are shown in Table 2. We use the Python package *emoji* [4] for demojizing emojis to emoji text.
A simple binary search approach to search the first position of emoji with maximum frequency was used and the corresponding algorithm is given in Algorithm 1. We use the first position of the most frequent emoji in a particular text because it is more likely to be associated with a context or with the user's intent to express an emotion. 0 represents MaxEmoji's occurrence towards the start of the text, 1 represents its occurrence in the middle, and 2 represents occurrence towards the end of the text.

Algorithm 1 Frequent Emoji Position and Intensity

```
procedure MAXPOSFREQ( text )
    ▷ Computing frequency of the most intense emoji and its first position of occurrence

    MaxEmoji = none
    MaxEmojiNumOccurence = -1
    MaxEmojiPos = -1
    length = len(text)
            ▷ Emoji List can be extracted by emoji Python package, which also gives start position of each emoji

▷ extract all emojis and their counts and store
    emojiDict = {emoji: count}
    emojiList = list of all emojis in text

    MaxEmojiNumOccurence =
                    max(emojiDict.count)
    MaxEmoji = extract first key with
                count as
            MaxEmojiNumOccurence
    startPos = first Occurrence of MaxEmoji
    mid = (length/2)
    if startPos ≥ 0 && startPos < mid/2 then
        ▷ Store 0 for occurrence of the emoji
        towards the start of the text
        maxPos = 0
    else if startPos ≥ mid/2 && startPos < (mid + length)/2 then
        ▷ Store 1 for occurrence of the emoji
        towards the middle of the text
        maxPos = 1
    else
        ▷ Store 2 for occurrence of the emoji
        towards the end of the text
        maxPos =2
                                ▷ end of procedure
```

3.4 Extracting Sentiment Scores

To determine if there is incongruence between the sentiment expressed by the text and that of the

[2]https://py-googletrans.readthedocs.io/en/latest/
[3]https://advertools.readthedocs.io/en/master/
[4]https://pypi.org/project/emoji/

Text	MaxEmoji	MaxEmoji#	MaxEmojiPos
"sameee 😂 and im canadian i didnt even know that one of the canadian artists was canadian 😂😂😂	😂	4	0
"6th hour is so boring 😴"	😴	1	2
"she just made my damn night😂😂😂😂😂😂😂 Here I am eating my husband like its so damn normal"	😂	7	1

Table 2: Emoji Occurrences and Positions

emoji sentiment scores were computed for both text and emojis using SentiWordNet, VADER, and TextBlob. The sentiment scores generally fall in the range of [-1,1] where negative scores indicate negative polarity and positive scores indicate positive polarity. Using these scores polarities of both text and corresponding emojis can be identified and compared for incongruence.
SentiWordNet (or SWN) qualifies WordNet synsets in Positive, Negative, and Objective labels by using numerical scores. VADER is a parsing rule-based model that is popularly used for sentiment analysis tasks. It uses lexical features, grammar, and syntax conventions of the language that express the intensity of sentiment. TextBlob is a Python library that contains many natural language processing tools. We used Python's NLTK interface [5] for all these three tools. We also used these tools to extract emoji scores of the emojis corresponding to the text. The emojis were demojized and their text description was passed to each of the above tools to compute emoji scores. In case an emoji was intense (i.e. more than one occurrence) its sentiment score was computing using the following methods.

1. On experimentation it was observed that appending *!* to a text increases the sentiment score of the text in direction of its polarity. Therefore, we appended *!* to the emoji text its Freq-1 times. i.e. if 😂 was used 3 times in a text, its demojized text along with intensity was "laughing with tears of joy!!"

2. SWN takes into account the number of PoS tags. These scores are added to compute the sentiment score of a sentence. When multiple emojis are used in a text, the demojized text of an emoji was concatenated as many times an emoji appeared with the text record in consideration. For instance 😂 appeared 3 times in a text, then the emoji text used to compute the sentiment score using SWN was "laughing with tears of joy laughing with tears of joy laughing with tears of joy".

The emoji sentiment scores were computed for all emojis in the text and added together to derive the final score of the emojis. We also computed the sentiment score of only the maximum occurring emoji using the above methods.
Emoji Sentiment Ranking (ESR) also gives the emoji sentiment score but it may not cater to recent emojis that have been added to the Unicode Consortium of emojis [6]. But these emojis may occur in SarcOji or any other text on social media. Thus, it was a challenge to apply ESR to all emojis. But, we observed that most of the frequent emojis in SarcOji texts were face emojis. Since, ESR also lists a large number of face emojis with their respective sentiment scores we used ESR, for computing the sentiment score of the most frequent emoji in the text. Sentiment scores of texts and emojis are computed as given in algorithm 2.

3.5 SarcOji Dataset

SarcOji Dataset is now available on github[7]. It comprises 5190 Facebook posts and 24187 Twitter tweets. The 'Sarcastic' labels for 'Text' from which the following features are derived as discussed as follows

- Emojis: List of emojis in the text
- MaxEmoji: Most frequent emoji in the text

[5]https://www.nltk.org/

[6]https://home.unicode.org/emoji/

[7]https://github.com/VanditaGroverKapila/SarcOji

Algorithm 2 Computing Text and Emoji Sentiment Scores

```
procedure SENTIMENT SCORES( cleanText, EmojiInfo)
  ▷ EmojInfo contains EmojiDict, MaxEmoji, MaxEmojiOccurence
      ▷ CleanText is text without any emojis, hyperlinks, mentions, or hashtags ▷ Compute sentiment scores for text using all the tools
    textVaderScore = vader(cleanText)
    textTextBlobScore = TextBlob(cleanText)
    textSWNScore = SWN(cleanText)

    esrMaxEmojiScore = esr(MaxEmoji)
    i = 0
    ScoreDict =
    {vader:0, textBlob:0 swn:0}
    for emoji in EmojiDict do
        emojiF = EmojiDict[emoji].count

  ▷ demojize is available in Python package
  that converts emoji to text

        emojiText = demojize(emoji)

        if emojiF ≥ 2 then
            Intensifier = !^(emojiF−1)
            concatIntensifier = Concatenate
                                 emojiText
                                 emojiF-1
                                 times
            exemojiText = emojiText
                             (concat with)
                             Intensifier
            semojiText = emojiText
                           (concat with)
                           concatIntensifier
      ▷ Computing sentiment scores of emoji
      Text using SWN, Vader, and TextBlob

            vaderEmojiScore =
                      vader(exemojiText)
            textBlobEmojiScore =
                      textBlob(exemojiText)
            sentiEmojiScoreI =
                  sentiWordnet(exemojiText)
            sentiEmojiScoreC =
               sentiWordnet(semojiText)
            sentiEmojiScore =
                    max(sentiEmojiScoreI,
                    sentiEmojiScoreC)
            Update ScoreDict
                                   ▷ end of procedure
```

Type	Number of Texts	Emoji Per Post	Intense Posts*
Sarcastic	11448	2.156	41.44%
Not Sarcastic	17929	1.526	22.98%

Table 3: SarcOji Dataset Statistics

- MaxEmojiNumOccurence: Frequency of MaxEmoji in the text.
- MaxEmojiPos: Position of MaxEmoji at Left, Middle, Right (0,1, or 2 respectively) from the text.
- TextSWN: Text sentiment score using SentiWordNet
- TextVader: Text sentiment score using VADER
- TextTextBlob: Text sentiment score using TextBlob
- EmojiSWN: Combined sentiment score of all emojis using SentiWordNet
- EmojiVader: Combined sentiment score of all emojis using VADER
- EmojiTextBlob: Combined sentiment score of all emojis using TextBlob
- MEmojiWN: Sentiment score of MaxEmoji using SentiWordNet
- MEVader: Sentiment score of MaxEmoji using VADER
- METB: Sentiment score of MaxEmoji using TextBlob
- ESR: Sentiment score of MaxEmoji using Emoji Sentiment Ranking

4 Observations and Inferences

In this section, we discuss some important Observations and Inferences after an in-depth analysis of the SarcOji dataset.

4.1 SarcOji Dataset Statstics

Table 3 provides the statistics for the compiled SarcOji dataset.[8]

The percentage of positive, neutral, and negative texts and emojis in SarcOji are reported in Figures 1 and 2.

[8] *Posts with >1 emojis

Text Type	SWN Text Sent	SWN Text %	SWN Emoji Sent	SWN Emoji %	VADER Text Sent	VADER Text %	VADER Emoji Sent	VADER Emoji %	TextBlob Text Sent	TextBlob Text %	TextBlob Emoji Sent	TextBlob Emoji %
Sarcastic	+ve	35.48	+ve	33.35	+ve	46.38	+ve	44.22	+ve	43.57	+ve	29.14
	neu	46.41	neu	55.62	neu	33.19	neu	45.12	neu	41.39	neu	63.02
	-ve	18.11	-ve	11.03	-ve	20.42	-ve	10.66	-ve	15.03	-ve	7.83

Figure 1: Sentiment Distribution in Sarcastic Texts

Text Type	SWN Text Sent	SWN Text %	SWN Emoji Sent	SWN Emoji %	VADER Text Sent	VADER Text %	VADER Emoji Sent	VADER Emoji %	TextBlob Text Sent	TextBlob Text %	TextBlob Emoji Sent	TextBlob Emoji %
Non Sarcastic	+ve	33.56	+ve	27.88	+ve	41.81	+ve	37.16	+ve	40.17	+ve	23.41
	neu	44.97	neu	45.75	neu	30.16	neu	29.17	neu	39.29	neu	44.88
	-ve	21.43	-ve	26.38	-ve	28.03	-ve	33.67	-ve	20.53	-ve	31.71

Figure 2: Sentiment Distribution in Non-Sarcastic Texts

It is observed from Figures 1 and 2 that in general there are more positive texts in sarcastic set. Also, the positive emojis are significantly more in the sarcastic set as compared to non-sarcastic texts. It is also important to observe that the neutral texts dominate in both sarcastic and non-sarcastic sets, which might make it difficult to determine incongruence.

4.2 Incongruence

To determine if there is incongruence between the polarity of text and the polarity of emojis we compare their sentiment scores. We consider incongruence when

- Polarity of text is +ve (>0) and that of emoji is -ve (<0)
- Polarity of text is -ve (<0) and that of emoji is +ve (>0)

Before comparing the sentiment scores for polarity, all the sentiment scores outside the range [-1,1] were normalized using a maximum absolute value scalar.

Sentiment scores computed by all methods for text and emojis are compared and reported in Table 4, 5, 6. All the numbers are reported in percentages.

Type	SWN	VADER	TextBlob
Sarcastic	9.79	12.87	7.55
Not Sarcastic	16.49	19.26	14.6

Table 4: Incongruence computed after taking into account all emoji scores

We see more agreement in Table 6 where the emoji sentiment score was computed using ESR for the MaxEmoji. Less incongruence between text and emojis was observed in the sarcastic text as compared to non-sarcastic texts. One of the reasons for this could be that neutral text and emojis are sig-

Type	SWN	VADER	TextBlob
Sarcastic	5.4	11.25	7.33
Not Sarcastic	9.5	18.43	15.11

Table 5: Incongruence computed after taking into account only the MaxEmoji score computed using SWN,VADER, and TextBlob

Type	SWN	VADER	TextBlob
Sarcastic	18.74	21.38	21.4
Not Sarcastic	21.32	22.8	21.8

Table 6: Incongruence computed after taking into account only the MaxEmoji score computed using Emoji Sentiment Ranking

nificantly high in the dataset. Thus, to understand sarcasm it is important to dive into neutral texts and emojis.

4.3 Emojis in SarcOji

In this section we report the emojis that were most used in the compiled SarcOji dataset. The top 25 emojis used in Sarcastic and Non-Sarcastic subsets of SarcOji are reported in Figures 3 and 4 respectively.

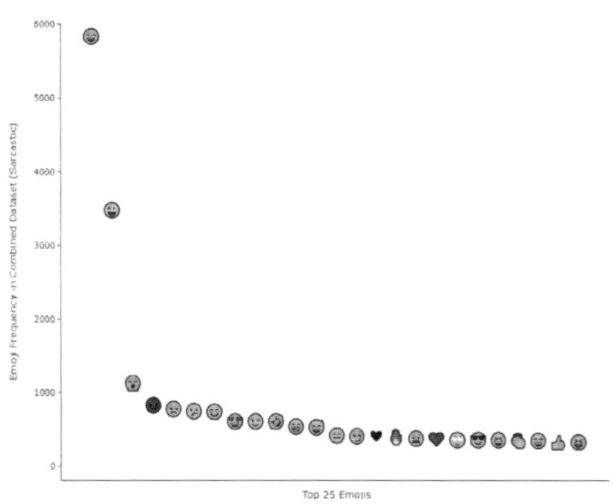

Figure 3: Sentiment Distribution in Sarcastic Texts

Usage in Text	😄	😜	😫	😡	😕
% of occurrence	18.763	***21.75***	2.43	1.05	0.08
Intensity (freq>1)	***50.14***	2.53	41.21	40	33.7

Table 7: Usage of Emojis in Sarcastic Texts

Usage in Text	😄	😜	😫	😡	😕
% of occurrence	19.342	0.45	15.16	13.04	13.02
Intensity (freq>1)	15.325	6.25	6.47	2.35	0.8

Table 8: Usage of Emojis in Non-Sarcastic Texts

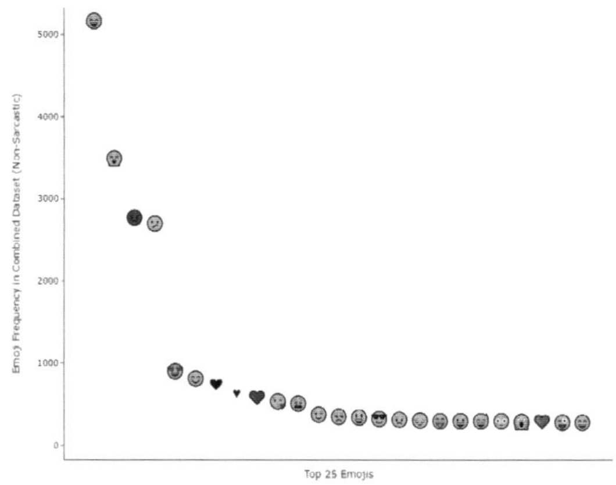

Figure 4: Sentiment Distribution in Non-Sarcastic Texts

😄 is the most popular emoji in SarcOji with 5669 occurences in 11448 sarcastic texts and 5018 occurences in 17929 sarcastic texts. This might be an indication that 😄 is one of the preferred emojis to express sarcasm.

4.4 Usage Patterns of Top Emojis

We further analyze usage patterns of the top-5 emojis of the entire SarcOji dataset in tables 7 and 8.

Some interesting observations can be made from Tables 7 and 8.
😄 is in general an emoji with maximum occurrences (frequency) in 18.76% of sarcastic texts. 19.34% of non-sarcastic texts also see 😄 as a MaxEmoji. But, 😄 is more intense in sarcastic texts. In 50% of sarcastic texts, the users have used 😄 more intensely. By intensity, we mean that an emoji is used repeatedly (more than 1 time) with the text in consideration. And in general, apart from 😜, all other emojis are used more intensely in sarcastic texts. It is to be noted that 😜 is the most dominant emoji in sarcastic texts which may

Tool	😂	😜	😭	😡	😕
	face with tears of joy	winking face with tongue	loudly crying face	Pouting face	Confused face
SWN	0.25	0.0	0.0	0.0	-0.5
VADER	0.44	0.0	-0.477	0.0	-0.4
TextBlob	0.8	0.0	-0.2	0.0	0.0
ESR	0.221	0.456	-0.093	-0.173	-0.4

Table 9: Sentiment scores of Emojis using various tools

Type	Left	Middle	Right
Sarcastic	13.75	18.88	67.36
Not Sarcastic	6.9	12.76	80.34

Table 10: Position of Occurrence of MaxEmoji (% of the text)

point towards its inherently sarcastic nature. This result is in alignment with (Thompson et al., 2016).

4.5 Sentiment Scores of Emojis

In table 9, the sentiment scores of the top-5 emojis computed using various tools used in this work are reported.

We observe that none of the tools agree with each other when it comes to computing the sentiment scores of the emojis. We also observe that SWN, VADER, and Textblob are computing sentiment scores as 0 for some emojis. This may impact determining the incongruence of text and emoji polarities. ESR is giving a more negative score for 😕 as compared to 😭.

Further work may be required that captures all the emojis (even those added every year). There is a need to build a tool that assigns and regularly updates numerical scores for emojis to identify the sentiment they express. For instance, 😂 may be associated more with a fun component when used non-sarcastically. But it may have a sarcastic connotation when it is used more intensely in a text.

4.6 Position of Occurrence of MaxEmoji

In Table 10 the percentages of texts where the MaxEmoji occurs first is provided. This trend is observed in the top-5 emojis also. The results of the position of emojis in non-sarcastic texts are similar to those reported by (Kralj Novak et al., 2015) and (Zhao et al., 2018) but vary significantly for sarcastic texts.

We can concur that users may use emojis in non-sarcastic texts towards the end to annotate or conclude their text. While in sarcastic texts they use emojis nearer to context.

5 Conclusion and Future Directions

In this work, we compiled a labeled sarcasm dataset SarcOji from five publicly available datasets. SarcOji contains 29377 labeled records with emojis. Sentiment scores were derived using SentiWordNet, VADER, and TextBlob for both text and emojis, and Emoji Sentiment Ranking was used to compute the sentiment score of MaxEmoji. Using this publicly available dataset, researchers can explore the role of emojis in sarcasm detection.

On studying SarcOji no significant incongruence between sarcastic text and corresponding emojis was found. But more exploration is needed to understand the role of seemingly neutral texts and emojis.

It was also observed that sarcastic texts, as well as emojis used with them, are more positive as compared to non-sarcastic texts.

😜 was the most used emoji in the sarcastic text. 😂 was frequently used in both sarcastic and non-sarcastic texts. In the sarcastic texts, 😂 was used more intensely (more occurrences in a single text). In general, the sarcastic subset of SarcOji saw double the number of texts with intense emojis as compared to the non-sarcastic subset. This means that the intensity of emojis used in the text can indicate sarcasm.

In 80% of non-sarcastic texts, the MaxEmoji appeared towards the end of the text. This number was 67.35% for sarcastic texts, while MaxEmoji appeared 18.9% times in the middle and 13.75% times towards the beginning of the text. This hints that emojis in sarcastic texts are more often used with the context.

With this work we have been able to identify that 😂 when used intensely may indicate sarcasm, while 😜 is inherently sarcastic in nature. We were also able to demonstrate that number and position of occurrence of an emoji in the text are strong indicators of sarcasm. Although not much incongruence in the polarity of sarcastic texts and emojis was observed, there is a need to understand the role of seemingly neutral text and emojis in discerning sarcasm.

In the future, existing emoji resources can be augmented to flag the sarcastic nature of emojis which can enable better training of sarcasm classifiers.

Acknowledgements

We thank all the researchers who have compiled and made Sarcasm datasets publicly and freely available. Compilation of SarcOji would not have been possible without these resources.

References

Ibrahim Abu Farha, Silviu Oprea, Steven Wilson, and Walid Magdy. 2022. SemEval-2022 Task 6: iSarcasmEval, Intended Sarcasm Detection in English and Arabic. In *Proceedings of the 16th International Workshop on Semantic Evaluation (SemEval-2022)*. Association for Computational Linguistics.

Stefano Baccianella, Andrea Esuli, and Fabrizio Sebastiani. 2010. SentiWordNet 3.0: An enhanced lexical resource for sentiment analysis and opinion mining. In *Proceedings of the Seventh International Conference on Language Resources and Evaluation (LREC'10)*, Valletta, Malta. European Language Resources Association (ELRA).

Andrea Esuli and Fabrizio Sebastiani. 2006. Sentiwordnet: A publicly available lexical resource for opinion mining. In *Proceedings of the fifth international conference on language resources and evaluation (LREC'06)*.

Bjarke Felbo, Alan Mislove, Anders Søgaard, Iyad Rahwan, and Sune Lehmann. 2017. Using millions of emoji occurrences to learn any-domain representations for detecting sentiment, emotion and sarcasm. *arXiv preprint arXiv:1708.00524*.

Charlotte Garcia, Alexandra Ţurcan, Hannah Howman, and Ruth Filik. 2022. Emoji as a tool to aid the comprehension of written sarcasm: Evidence from younger and older adults. *Computers in Human Behavior*, 126:106971.

Aniruddha Ghosh and Tony Veale. 2016. Fracking sarcasm using neural network. In *Proceedings of the 7th workshop on computational approaches to subjectivity, sentiment and social media analysis*, pages 161–169.

Aniruddha Ghosh and Tony Veale. 2017. Magnets for sarcasm: Making sarcasm detection timely, contextual and very personal. In *Proceedings of the 2017 Conference on Empirical Methods in Natural Language Processing*, pages 482–491.

Debanjan Ghosh, Alexander Richard Fabbri, and Smaranda Muresan. 2017. The role of conversation context for sarcasm detection in online interactions. *arXiv preprint arXiv:1707.06226*.

Debanjan Ghosh, Avijit Vajpayee, and Smaranda Muresan. 2020. A report on the 2020 sarcasm detection shared task. *arXiv preprint arXiv:2005.05814*.

Raymond W Gibbs Jr, John S Leggitt, and Elizabeth A Turner. 2002. What's special about figurative language in emotional communication? In *The verbal communication of emotions*, pages 133–158. Psychology Press.

Vandita Grover. 2021. Exploiting emojis in sentiment analysis: A survey. *Journal of The Institution of Engineers (India): Series B*, pages 1–14.

Devamanyu Hazarika, Soujanya Poria, Sruthi Gorantla, Erik Cambria, Roger Zimmermann, and Rada Mihalcea. 2018. Cascade: Contextual sarcasm detection in online discussion forums. *arXiv preprint arXiv:1805.06413*.

Clayton Hutto and Eric Gilbert. 2014. Vader: A parsimonious rule-based model for sentiment analysis of social media text. In *Proceedings of the international AAAI conference on web and social media*, volume 8, pages 216–225.

Adarsh M J and Pushpa Ravikumar. 2019. Sarcasm detection in text data to bring out genuine sentiments for sentimental analysis. In *2019 1st International Conference on Advances in Information Technology (ICAIT)*, pages 94–98.

Amit Kumar Jena, Aman Sinha, and Rohit Agarwal. 2020. C-net: contextual network for sarcasm detection. In *Proceedings of the Second Workshop on Figurative Language Processing*, pages 61–66.

Aditya Joshi, Pushpak Bhattacharyya, and Mark J Carman. 2017. Automatic sarcasm detection: A survey. *ACM Computing Surveys (CSUR)*, 50(5):1–22.

Aditya Joshi, Pushpak Bhattacharyya, and Mark J Carman. 2018. Sarcasm detection using incongruity within target text. In *Investigations in Computational Sarcasm*, pages 59–91. Springer.

Aditya Joshi, Vinita Sharma, and Pushpak Bhattacharyya. 2015. Harnessing context incongruity for sarcasm detection. In *Proceedings of the 53rd Annual Meeting of the Association for Computational Linguistics and the 7th International Joint Conference on Natural Language Processing (Volume 2: Short Papers)*, pages 757–762.

Mikhail Khodak, Nikunj Saunshi, and Kiran Vodrahalli. 2017. A large self-annotated corpus for sarcasm. *arXiv preprint arXiv:1704.05579*.

Petra Kralj Novak, Jasmina Smailović, Borut Sluban, and Igor Mozetič. 2015. Sentiment of emojis. *PLOS ONE*, 10(12):1–22.

Hannah Miller, Daniel Kluver, Jacob Thebault-Spieker, Loren Terveen, and Brent Hecht. 2017. Understanding emoji ambiguity in context: The role of text in emoji-related miscommunication. In *Proceedings of the International AAAI Conference on Web and Social Media*, volume 11, pages 152–161.

Silviu Oprea and Walid Magdy. 2019. isarcasm: A dataset of intended sarcasm. *arXiv preprint arXiv:1911.03123*.

Md Saifullah Razali, Alfian Abdul Halin, Noris Mohd Norowi, and Shyamala C Doraisamy. 2017. The importance of multimodality in sarcasm detection for sentiment analysis. In *2017 IEEE 15th Student Conference on Research and Development (SCOReD)*, pages 56–60. IEEE.

Aanshi Rustagi, Annapurna Jonnalagadda, Aswani Kumar Cherukuri, and Amir Ahmad. 2022. *Toward Sarcasm Detection in Reviews—A Dual Parametric Approach with Emojis and Ratings*, pages 245–257. Springer Singapore, Singapore.

Jayashree Subramanian, Varun Sridharan, Kai Shu, and Huan Liu. 2019. Exploiting emojis for sarcasm detection. In *International Conference on Social Computing, Behavioral-Cultural Modeling and Prediction and Behavior Representation in Modeling and Simulation*, pages 70–80. Springer.

Karthik Sundararajan, J. Vijay Saravana, and Anandhakumar Palanisamy. 2021. Textual feature ensemble-based sarcasm detection in twitter data. In *Intelligence in Big Data Technologies—Beyond the Hype*, pages 443–450, Singapore. Springer Singapore.

Kavita Tewani. 2019. Sarcasm detection using multiple occurrences of emojis and hashtagged words. In *International Conference on Advances in Computational Intelligence and Informatics*, pages 81–87. Springer.

Dominic Thompson, Ian G Mackenzie, Hartmut Leuthold, and Ruth Filik. 2016. Emotional responses to irony and emoticons in written language: Evidence from eda and facial emg. *Psychophysiology*, 53(7):1054–1062.

Yin Wang, Xuyang Xu, Ziteng Gao, and Xi Shi. 2021. A prior probability of speaker information and emojis embedding approach to sarcasm detection. In *2021 IEEE International Conference on Engineering, Technology Education (TALE)*, pages 1033–1038.

Sanjaya Wijeratne, Lakshika Balasuriya, Amit Sheth, and Derek Doran. 2017a. Emojinet: An open service and api for emoji sense discovery. In *Proceedings of the International AAAI Conference on Web and Social Media*, volume 11, pages 437–446.

Sanjaya Wijeratne, Lakshika Balasuriya, Amit Sheth, and Derek Doran. 2017b. A semantics-based measure of emoji similarity. In *Proceedings of the International Conference on Web Intelligence*, pages 646–653.

Peijun Zhao, Jia Jia, Yongsheng An, Jie Liang, Lexing Xie, and Jiebo Luo. 2018. Analyzing and predicting emoji usages in social media. In *Companion Proceedings of the The Web Conference 2018*, pages 327–334.

Conducting Cross-Cultural Research on COVID-19 Memes

Jing Ge-Stadnyk
University of California, Berkeley
California, USA
jingge@berkeley.edu

Lusha Sa
South-Central University for Nationalities
Wuhan, China
3089508@mail.scuec.edu.cn

Abstract

A cross-linguistic study of COVID-19 memes should allow scholars and professionals to gain insight into how people engage in socially and politically important issues and how culture has influenced societal responses to the global pandemic. This preliminary study employs framing analysis to examine and compare issues, actors and stances conveyed by both English and Chinese memes. The overall findings point to divergence in the way individuals communicate pandemic-related issues in English-speaking countries versus China, although a few similarities were also identified. 'Regulation' is the most common issue addressed by both English and Chinese memes, though the latter does so at a comparatively higher rate. The 'ordinary people' image within these memes accounts for the largest percentage in both data sets. Although both Chinese and English memes primarily express negative emotions, the former often occurs on an interpersonal level, whereas the latter aims at criticizing society and certain group of people in general. Lastly, this study proposes explanations for these findings in terms of culture and political environment.

1 Introduction

While memes have provided people worldwide with a unique way to engage in the pandemic discourse through expressing opinions and values, voicing complex feelings, and seeking out affiliations with others (Outley et al., 2020; Flecha Ortiz et al., 2021), a systematic examination of their use across cultures has not been subject to comparative analysis. The premise of this paper is that a communication-oriented study of COVID-memes will provide scholars and professionals (e.g., policy makers) with a route to understanding a key device many now use to engage with socially and politically important issues. These individual and collective narratives can be highly consequential for users' mental health and emotional well-being (de Saint Laurent et al., 2021). They can also impact public confidence and trust in the various preventive measures being implemented, as well as the institutions responsible for adopting them. Moreover, a comparative account of meme use across cultures should shed light on fundamental questions about the importance of culture in societal responses to the global pandemic. As (Kubba, 2020) convincingly argues, "with our attention focused on scientific and technological innovations in response to COVID-19, there is much missed with respect to cultural innovation during this time."

This preliminary study employs a framing analysis to comparably examine the pandemic-related English and Chinese memes as collected from *memebase*[1] and *Dou Tu La*[2] website respectively. We analyze issues, actors and actors' stances conveyed by the sample memes. Given the difficulty to distinguish between the geopolitical origins of online content, users employ language to establish borders while consuming such content. Therefore, viewing language as an analogue to culture is a feasible approach to cross-cultural research on digital content (Nissenbaum and Shifman, 2018).

2 Background

2.1 Operating the Concept of Culture

We operationalize culture, i.e., a frame of reference consisting of shared beliefs, values, and norms in varying degrees in a group (Hofstede, 1980), as national identity by focusing on the dichotomy of individualism and collectivism. National culture, which operates as a social control mechanism, influences actions of individuals and groups in times of crisis the pandemic (Kubba, 2020). This perspective is anchored in protection efficacy achieved within different cultures. Members of individualistic cultures (e.g., Americans) tend to prioritize

[1] https://memebase.cheezburger.com/
[2] https://www.pkdoutu.com/

Proceedings of the The Fifth International Workshop on Emoji Understanding and Applications in Social Media, pages 40 - 46
July 14, 2022 ©2022 Association for Computational Linguistics

their own privacy and freedom, whereas those from collectivistic cultures (e.g., Chinese) often believe the willingness and capability of their community to protect themselves and therefore can achieve the massive social coordination (Logan, 2020).

Since Internet memes' articulation serves as both creations of groups and spaces for personal expression, this outlet allows users worldwide to express their opinions and shape the mindsets (Abidin, 2020; de Saint Laurent et al., 2021; MacDonald, 2021). Therefore, theoretically at least, the ways English and Chinese memes communicate the pandemic display similarities and differences due to different cultural contexts. However, this assumption has not been subjected to systematic research yet.

2.2 Internet Memes and the Pandemic

Since Internet memes convey visual arguments reflecting certain ideological practices (Nissenbaum and Shifman, 2018), people from different countries often employ them to express their values and opinions in the digital sphere. For example, digital anthropologists find that people in Italy use both serious and humorous memes to promote certain values and make fun of others; users in Trinidad and Chile tend to employ memes to comment on both social and personal issues; while Chinese who do not want to broadcast or share personal opinions in the offline domain often use memes to voice complex feelings (Miller). The aforementioned literature suggests that a discourse study of memes allows for a better understanding of differing public opinions of, and responses to, the global pandemic.

The literature on COVID-19 memes has primarily focused on their different uses in specific cultural contexts. The first line of research looked at how individuals employ these memes as a form of coping strategy. For instance, studies focusing on Spanish-speaking social media (Flecha Ortiz et al., 2021) and Kenya (Oduor and Kodak, 2020) identified meme use as collective coping. Research focusing on Singapore and Malaysia found that social media users often employ pandemic memes to enhance public awareness on specific issues, prescribe behaviors, and shape mindsets in the public arena (Abidin, 2020).

The second line of research has focused on meme use across social media platforms as social-political commentary. For instance, Reddit users and Indonesians on Instagram employ COVID-19 memes to criticize the incompetence of political leaders while highlighting those who either do or do not respect established measures (de Saint Laurent et al., 2021). Twitter users adopt pandemic memes to reclaim black power (Outley); Gen Xers use memes to claim that they can deal with the pandemic and to point out that other generations did not take self-isolation as seriously as they should have (MacDonald, 2021).

In contrast, cross-cultural research on COVID-19 memes has received less attention. One study (Chuanzhao et al., 2020) compared the perception of COVID-19 memes by young people in Russia and China, showing that both groups appreciate memes encompassing certain qualities (e.g., relevance, kindness, cheerfulness). However, Chinese respondents strive for orderliness and consensus, whereas Russians show a tendency towards polarization of opinion with a focus on individualism. The other study investigating COVID-19 misinformation conveyed by memes in China, the United States, and Iran, suggesting that pandemic-related misinformation varies significantly across countries depending on their particular culture, beliefs/religions, the robustness of freedom of speech and the power of citizens vis-a'-vis the government (Madraki et al., 2021). For example, lower rates of misinformation on Chinese social media are likely due to strict control by the Chinese government.

Building on the above-mentioned literature, we argue that COVID-19 memes convey important information regarding specific public's opinions; the ways these memes communicate the pandemic exhibit similarities and differences according to cultural context. To explore this premise systematically, this study sought to address the following research question: How do English and Chinese memes communicate the COVID-19 pandemic via the Internet?

3 Methodology

3.1 Data

We compared COVID-19 memes in two languages that can represent diverse cultures (Nissenbaum and Shifman, 2018): English and Chinese. The data comprise English memes collected on *memebase*[3] and *Dou Tu La*[4]. These two websites can

[3] https://memebase.cheezburger.com/

[4] https://www.pkdoutu.com/

be seen as a mainstreamed space for meme curation, and therefore, constitute a suitable source for outlining the framing elements of the pandemic memes.

The first author manually collected the first 80 English memes presented on the webpage by searching 'COVID memes' and 'pandemic memes', and then selected the first 80 Chinese memes by searching two phases describing coronavirus memes (i.e., 冠状病毒表情包; 冠状病毒图片) In total, the data comprise 160 examples. This size is considered effective for a manual coding study (Kolbe and Burnett, 1991).

3.2 Method of Analysis

Framing analysis allows this study to identify communication patterns of pandemic memes across different cultures, because it communicates an event (such as the pandemic) through selection, exclusion, and emphasis (Entman, 1993). Moreover, frames highlight a certain piece of information about an event, making it more noticeable, meaningful, and memorable to audiences. In other words, framing analysis will allow this study to identify key information about COVID-19 as perpetuated in both English and Chinese memes. Specifically, the study focuses on three essential framing elements: 1) issues addressed by pandemic memes; 2) the actors involved in these issues (i.e. people either referred to in a meme or represented in indirect speech); and, 3) actors' stances towards said issues (what idea, opinion, criticism, etc. is being conveyed).

We used a combination of content analysis and descriptive statistical analysis. We followed the principles of the grounded theory approach. In line with later developments in this approach (Nissenbaum and Shifman, 2018), the interpretative process also considered conceptual categories mentioned in the literature review section. Thus, the identified categories stemmed from previous studies and were in conjunction with new observations obtained in the course of analysis.

The first author and a research assistant used 10 examples that were not included in the data to practice coding. Next, we coded a sample set comprising 25 English and 25 Chinese memes to establish inter-coder reliability. The coding of issues conveyed by the sample memes was conducted by identifying specific topics based on content analysis, followed by collapsing and combining similar concepts based on conceptual similarities to derive logical groupings. Actors involved in these pandemic-related issues were coded based on people and groups of people that were either referred to in the meme or that were represented in indirect speech (e.g., 'ordinary people,' 'politicians,' 'medical workers'). Common objects as well as art objects (e.g., paintings) were coded in the category 'other.' Finally, stance was coded according to 'positive' and 'negative' based on Ekman's basic emotions[5]. Final inter-reliability scores (Scott's pi) were high: Issues (0.91), actors (0.93), and stance (0.82). The principal investigator coded the rest of the data, while consulting the research assistant to clarify, validate and comment on the main interpretations.

4 Findings and Discussion

The results of the research question support the working premise of this study; namely, that memes convey respective public's opinions and that culture influences how people have been responding to the pandemic.

4.1 Issues Addressed by COVID-19 Memes

We found that both English and Chinese memes address issues relating to 'regulation,' 'scarcity of supplies,' and 'work and study.' 'Regulation' (i.e., rules/preventive measures issued by government institutions) accounts for the largest overall percentage of the identified issues in Chinese and English data groups (56% and 37% respectively, example 1 (Appendix: Figure 1) and 2 (Appendix: Figure 2)). This result aligns with (Norstrom and Sarna, 2021)'s study focusing on COVID-19 memes in Poland, showing that 'bans and orders' is the most prominent issue. This result can be explained by the framing theory: people across cultures tend to use internet memes to emphasize the most pressing challenges brought about by the pandemic (e.g., sheltering-in-place, social distancing). Also noteworthy is that the Chinese memes addressed the 'regulation' issue more often than did the English memes. This result can be explained by the fact that, compared to Western countries, China's coronavirus crackdown has involved more surveillance and tighter controls (Kuo, 2020). As a result, the series of regulations issued and implemented by Chinese authorities have likely posed greater challenges for Chinese citizens than have

[5]https://www.paulekman.com/universal-emotions/

comparable government measures posed for people in the West.

'Work and study' is the second most common issue conveyed by the English memes (18%) (example 3 (Appendix: Figure 3)), followed by 'viewing 2020 as a bad year' (17%) (example 4 (Appendix: Figure 4)) and 'vaccine' (13%). In contrast, the first issue occurred less often in Chinese memes. This can be explained by the notion that people from individualistic cultures stress personal goals and matters (Kubba, 2020). Issues relating to bad year and vaccine are absent in the Chinese data. The second most prominent issue (i.e., 'fighting the virus' or showing their determination to crack down on the virus, example 5 (Appendix: Figure 5)) (21%) in Chinese memes suggests that people hailing from collectivistic cultures focus more on group goals. The absence of issues regarding 'virus escalation,' 'politics' and 'unemployment and economy' in Chinese data might be due to a lack of freedom of speech coupled with strict media censorship in China, since these issues relate to negative news and sensitive topics.

4.2 Actors Involved in the Issues

We identified that actors involved in both English and Chinese memes include 'ordinary people' (77% and 79% respectively) and 'medical worker' (1% and 3.8% respectively). Interestingly, we observed that while English memes often used celebrities (e.g., movie and TV actors and singers) to refer to ordinary people, Chinese memes largely employed popular Internet characters (such as 'Panda Man' or person with a panda-like head, and 'a girl with mushroom-shaped head') to refer to a particular actor. This result is consistent with (Norstrom and Sarna, 2021)'s study focusing on COVID-19 meme use in Poland, which showed that 'ordinary men' is the most prominent actor. While the unique categories identified in the English memes are 'politician,' (9%), 'media figures,' (3%), and 'animal' (3%), those found in the Chinese memes are 'authority,' (4.9%), and 'humanized virus,' (9.8%).

While Chinese memes employed 'medical workers' to address the importance of adhering to regulations, English memes used this actor to reveal the escalation of the virus. The results can be explained by China's cultural and societal norms, that is, the strong emphasis on harmonious relationships and cooperation among community members (Ge-Stadnyk, 2021). Furthermore, one commonly used actor among the English memes (i.e. 'politician') is absent in the Chinese data. That is, Chinese are taught, and expected, to respect and obey the country's officials and are not allowed to poke fun at them through, for example, the use of memes (Madraki et al., 2021).

4.3 Stances Conveyed by the Pandemic Memes

We found both positive and negative emotions across the sample images. Negative emotions (e.g., anger, sadness, disappointment) were the most prominent stance found in English and Chinese memes (81% and 83% respectively). We thus have an overall negative skew. While the sample memes expressing positive emotions (e.g., amusement) were notably plain and direct, those conveying anger and sadness were nuanced and indirect. We observed that anger embedded in Chinese memes primarily occurs on an interpersonal level (i.e., reference to specific individuals, example 6 (Appendix: Figure 6)), whereas anger in English memes often aims at criticizing society and certain group of people in general (e.g., Gen Z, example 7 (Appendix: Figure 7)).

Drawing on Nissenbaum and Shifman (2018)'s work, we observed that sadness embedded in the memes conveys 'sarcastic pity,' 'earnest fail,' and 'pathetic loss.' Interestingly, meme users (especially Chinese) express sadness by depicting their own social embarrassments, daily struggles and failures (e.g., weight gain) (i.e., earnest fail, example 8 (Appendix: Figure 8)) and by manifesting pathetic loss (i.e., sadness is felt over trivial or mundane inconveniences). Although English memes also conveyed these nuanced emotions, they also often express sarcastic pity (i.e., berating people by sarcastically expressing pity over perceived failures or incompetency, example 9 (Appendix: Figure 9)).

These observations can also be explained through a cultural lens. As (Kubba, 2020) asserts, citizens holding individualistic worldviews tend to reject government interference and trust their immediate social networks. However, people from collectivistic cultures often find strength in bonding with both their own governments and the larger citizenry.

4.4 Theoretical and Practical Implications

First, this study broadens CMC literature by examining internet memes from a communication-oriented perspective. Second, while previous research employed framing analysis to investigate communication in political and media discourse, this study has used it to examine user-generated content. Finally, this paper's results can inform future research aimed at better understanding how cultural and social environments influence people responding to crises.

Further, the empirical findings derived from this study can be useful for media scholars, psychologists, and policymakers who are interested in memes and online narratives. Based on this study's findings, one can assert that coronavirus memes not only reflect a harsh reality at the personal and societal levels, but also lend support for, or express strong disapproval of, specific belief systems and courses of action.

Acknowledgements

This research is funded by National Social Science Fund of China (NSSFC), GSY16015.

References

Crystal Abidin. 2020. Meme factory cultures and content pivoting in singapore and malaysia during covid-19. *The Harvard Kennedy School Misinformation Review*, 1:1–20.

Lin Chuanzhao, Steblovskaia So, et al. 2020. Psychological and ethnocultural sensitivities in the perception of covid-19 memes by young people in russia and china. *Psychology in Russia: State of the art*, 13(4):148–167.

Constance de Saint Laurent, Vlad P Glăveanu, and Ioana Literat. 2021. Internet memes as partial stories: Identifying political narratives in coronavirus memes. *Social Media+ Society*, 7(1):1–13.

Robert M Entman. 1993. Framing: Towards clarification of a fractured paradigm. *McQuail's reader in mass communication theory*, pages 390–397.

José A Flecha Ortiz, Maria A Santos Corrada, Evelyn Lopez, and Virgin Dones. 2021. Analysis of the use of memes as an exponent of collective coping during covid-19 in puerto rico. *Media International Australia*, 178(1):168–181.

Jing Ge-Stadnyk. 2021. Communicative functions of emoji sequences in the context of self-presentation: A comparative study of weibo and twitter users. *Discourse & Communication*, 15(4):369–387.

Geert Hofstede. 1980. *Culture's consequences: International differences in work-related values*, volume 5. sage.

Richard H Kolbe and Melissa S Burnett. 1991. Content-analysis research: An examination of applications with directives for improving research reliability and objectivity. *Journal of consumer research*, 18(2):243–250.

S Kubba. 2020. The importance of culture in societal responses to covid-19. *Harvard Political Review*.

Lily Kuo. 2020. More surveillance, tighter controls: China's coronavirus crackdown.

Jim Logan. 2020. How different societies react to pandemics?

Shana MacDonald. 2021. What do you (really) meme? pandemic memes as social political repositories. *Leisure Sciences*, 43(1-2):143–151.

Golshan Madraki, Isabella Grasso, Jacqueline M. Otala, Yu Liu, and Jeanna Matthews. 2021. Characterizing and comparing covid-19 misinformation across languages, countries and platforms. In *Companion Proceedings of the Web Conference 2021*, pages 213–223.

Daniel Miller. Memes have become the moral police of online life.

Asaf Nissenbaum and Limor Shifman. 2018. Meme templates as expressive repertoires in a globalizing world: A cross-linguistic study. *Journal of Computer-Mediated Communication*, 23(5):294–310.

Roza Norstrom and Pawel Sarna. 2021. Internet memes in covid-19 lockdown times in poland. *Comunicar*, 29(67).

Juliet Atieno Oduor and Benard Kodak. 2020. Online humour as a coping mechanism in the face of corona virus pandemic: The kenyan context. *East African Scholars Journal of Psychology and Behavioural Sciences*, 2(4):1–8.

Corliss Outley, Shamaya Bowen, and Harrison Pinckney. 2020. Laughing while black: Resistance, coping and the use of humor as a pandemic pastime among blacks. *Leisure Sciences*, 43(1-2):305–314.

A Appendix: Examples for COVID-19 Memes

Figure 1: Example 1

Figure 2: Example 2 - Text Translation: This is how I look at home.

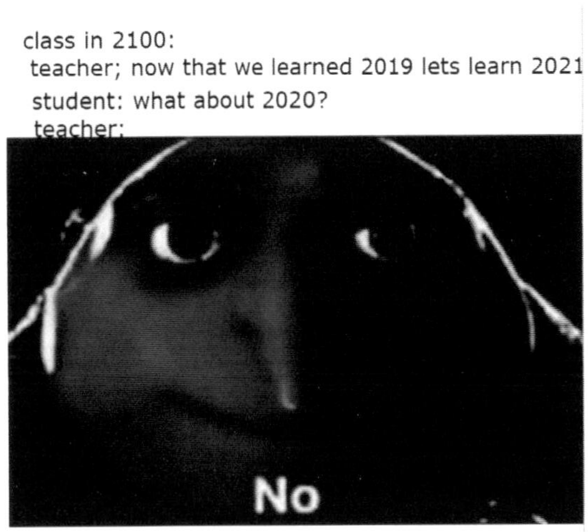

Figure 3: Example 3

Figure 4: Example 4

Figure 5: Example 5 - Text Translation: Not dining together is healthiest.

.

Figure 6: Example 6 - Text Translation: I am going to poison you to death.

.

Figure 7: Example 7

.

Figure 8: Example 8

.

Figure 9: Example 9

.

Investigating the Influence of Users Personality on the Ambiguous Emoji Perception

Olga Iarygina
University of Copenhagen
olia@di.ku.dk

Abstract

Emojis are an integral part of Internet communication nowadays. Even though, they are supposed to make the text clearer and less dubious, some emojis are ambiguous and can be interpreted in different ways. One of the factors that determine the perception of emojis is the user's personality. In this work, I conducted an experimental study and investigated how personality traits, measured with a Big Five Inventory (BFI) questionnaire, affect reaction time when interpreting emoji. For a set of emoji, for which there are several possible interpretations, participants had to determine whether the emoji fits the presented context or not. Using regression analysis, I found that conscientiousness and neuroticism significantly predict the reaction time the person needs to decide about the emoji. More conscientious people take longer to resolve ambiguity, while more neurotic people make decisions about ambiguous emoji faster. The knowledge of the relationship between personality and emoji interpretation can lead to effective use of knowledge of people's characters in personalizing interactive computer systems.

1 Introduction

Emojis have become incredibly popular on the Internet (Kralj Novak et al., 2015; Pavalanathan and Eisenstein, 2015). One reason for that is that text messaging is one of the most common communication channels now. But yet being convenient and enabling communication at a distance, text communication is not as expressive as live speech (Lengel and Daft, 1984). Since we can read the text with different intonations, text messages can be easily misunderstood. Emojis, which are pictograms depicting human faces, gestures and objects, partially solve this problem by augmenting text with emotional awareness cues.

However, despite being the visual representation, emoji can have the same ambiguity as words at the lexical meaning level (Prada et al., 2016; Cunha et al., 2020). Even though usually emoji are used within the context, which in theory should work well in both directions: emoji complement and resolve the ambiguity of the text, and the emoji itself in conjunction with the text should not cause difficulties in interpretation, it doesn't always work. And for different reasons, the same emoji can be interpreted differently by different people.

One of the plain explanations is that emoji rendering is specific to different operating systems, for example, for Apple and Google smartphones, and the same emoji can look quite different on different devices. Moreover, operating systems update rendering with newer versions and even users of the same device and platform may see slightly different emojis depending on whether they have updated their software or not. Finally, emojis diverge on different platforms. For example, Facebook uses a fairly specific rendering, quite different from the basic one. Of course, this affects how people perceive the same emoji and can have an impact on communication (Miller et al., 2017).

However, the perception of emojis can depend not only on the technical characteristics of the device but also on the person using them. Research shows that how a person interprets emojis is influenced by age, gender, cultural background (Barbieri et al., 2016; Jaeger et al., 2017; Wolf, 2000). But most studies address the issue of flattering differences at the level of group characteristics, and not many research analyze the influence of user personality on the interpretation of emoji. The existing ones mainly analyze emojis isolated from the context (Völkel et al., 2019). While taking into account that we usually see emojis as complementary to the text, it is important to analyze them within the context.

Thus, in this work, I'm trying to touch on this gap, and understand if there is a connection between the personality of the user and the way he

Proceedings of the The Fifth International Workshop on Emoji Understanding and Applications in Social Media, pages 47 - 62
July 14, 2022

perceives emoji within the text context - in the form in which we usually see emoji. So my research question is: *Do personality traits have an impact on how people perceive ambiguous emojis in context?*

To address these questions, I conducted an experimental study in which I presented people with ambiguous emoji, for which two more or less equivalent contexts are possible, and measured the time it took for them to decide whether the presented emoji fits the context or not. The participants then completed a BFI survey to determine their personality profiles. Finally, using regression analysis, I tested if there is a significant effect of different personality traits on reaction time when resolving emoji ambiguity.

My results show that conscientiousness and neuroticism significantly predict the reaction time the person needs to decide about the emoji. More conscientious people take longer to resolve ambiguity, while more neurotic people make decisions about ambiguous emoji faster. The interaction with the context presented affects the impact of both conscientiousness and neuroticism on the reaction time.

Thus, the contributions of this work are as follows: First, I try to address the gap in the studies of the link between user personality and emoji interpretation. Second, this study explores how people with different personalities perceive not standalone but emojis in context as we usually see them in text messaging. Finally, to my knowledge, existing research examines the perception of emoji in terms of choosing a qualitative interpretation, while I measure the relationship between personality and perception of emotional ambiguity by measuring reaction time.

2 Theoretical Background

2.1 Why do we use emoji?

When we speak in person, our language is enriched with non-verbal cues such as facial expressions, gestures and intonation (Burgoon et al., 2010). However, text messaging, despite its advantages as the ability to communicate at a distance and respond at a convenient time, is devoid of a non-verbal communication channel. From this, the sender and the recipient can intonate and interpret the same text in different ways, which can cause misunderstanding (Aoki and Woodruff, 2005). One possible way to mitigate this problem is by using emoji - pictograms that reflect facial expressions, gestures, or objects (Derks et al., 2008). They can serve as a replacement for gestures or emotions of the interlocutor and thereby make the text less ambiguous.

Lo discovered that the same text could be understood in different ways, depending on which emoticon is placed after it (Lo, 2008; Walther, 2011). Walther and D'Addario, on the one hand, found that, in general, the emotional colouring of the text itself is more important for interpretation than the emoticons. However, in the case of emoticons displaying negative emotions, the interpretation of the text changed significantly (Walther, 2011).

Thus, among the most common reasons found as the result of qualitative research, people use emojis to heighten the emotional colouring of the text (Hu et al., 2017). Another reason is to clarify the tone of the initially neutral message. For example, as a result of interviewing people, Cramer et al. found that people can add "heart" or "kiss" to add a romantic context to the neutral message ("See you 😘") (Cramer et al., 2016). Sometimes emojis add situational meaning, for example, "I am travelling to Germany next week ✈️," explaining that person will go to Germany by plane (Kaye et al., 2016). Another common reason to use emojis is to lighten the tone of the message and make people perceive aggressive messages more positively (Kaye et al., 2016; Rodrigues et al., 2017). Lastly, a few studies mention the emoji's function as referring to shared memories and jokes and increasing intimacy and closeness between people (Kaye et al., 2016; Kelly and Watts, 2015; Rodrigues et al., 2017).

2.2 Lexical Ambiguity

The phenomenon of lexical ambiguity, when a single word has multiple meanings, is quite common in the language (Beekhuizen et al., 2021). It is a natural feature of any language allowing the expression of multiple concepts within a limited vocabulary (Youn et al., 2016). Since humans are able to effectively decode this ambiguity and process multiple senses of a single word, research on lexical ambiguity occupies one of the key places in the cognitive sciences of language.

Despite the fact that emoji should be more univocal (Prada et al., 2016; Cunha et al., 2020), since they are a visual representation of concepts, ambiguity occurs in them too (Kralj Novak et al., 2015). In written text, emojis perform the function of replacing non-verbal communication methods such as facial expressions and gestures. And, given this essence, most often, emojis are used not separately but within the context, in which they should be perceived as a whole (Bavelas and Chovil, 2000). In the same manner, as we perceive the interlocutor, who gestures and expresses emotions during speech.

The problem of emoji ambiguity is approached from different angles. There are several dictionaries constructed with the aim of collecting a base of meanings associated with emoji and potentially disambiguating them. For example, Wijeratne et al. created a semantic tool, EmojiNet, allowing systems to link emojis with their meaning in context, which was successfully tested on disambiguating context in Twitter (Wijeratne et al., 2016, 2017). They also looked at the 25 most commonly misused emojis when applying the emoji sense disambiguation algorithm. In a similar manner, Novak and colleagues came up with a sentiment vocabulary for emoji based on the representations of tweets in which emoji appear (Kralj Novak et al., 2015). However, Miller argues that such solutions are not effective because people often disagree on the interpretation of the same emoji (Miller et al., 2017).

2.3 Perception of emojis

There can be several reasons for the fact that people can interpret the same emoji in different ways. Some of them are technical in nature and are related to the essence of emoji as such. Emojis are Unicode icons, and the way they are displayed depends on the operating system, its version and the platform on which they are used (Miller et al., 2016; Davis and Holbrook). So, for example, emoji in Apple and Android can be significantly different. Moreover, with software updates, manufacturers update emoji as well, so even people with the same phones but with an updated and not updated OS version can see different displays of the same emoji. Finally, there are platforms like Facebook that have their own emoji renderings (Miller et al., 2017).

Apart from technical factors, there are also human-related factors. Tigwell and Flatla found that users can perceive the sentiment of emoji differently even when they are shown on the same device and platform (Tigwell and Flatla, 2016). The way a person interprets emojis was found to be influenced by age (Jaeger et al., 2017; Koch et al., 2022). Herring et al. show that people over 30 have a tendency to interpret emojis too literally and younger people understand them in a more conventional manner (Herring and Dainas, 2020). Regarding gender, females have generally more positive attitudes towards emojis use (Chen et al., 2018), and females use more variations of emojis (Prada et al., 2018), mostly to express positive feelings such as support and joy. Males in general use emotions more to express teasing and sarcasm (Wolf, 2000). Finally, miscommunication in emojis can also be explained by cultural factors, and emojis can be interpreted differently in regards to the socio-geographics of a country. Barbieri et al. found that people from the UK and Spain have disagreements in the interpretation of weather-related emojis, and people from the UK and the USA perceive emoji related to holidays differently (Barbieri et al., 2016).

2.4 User personality and emoji use

The above-mentioned studies, explore differences in perception at the group level, and there is currently not a lot of research addressing the difference in emoji perception at the individual level. This aspect may be quite important because it is known that personality affects the way people express themselves, raising the assumption that it may also influence how people interpret emotions (Campbell and Rushton, 1978; Costa and McCrae, 1980). Li et al. examined the influence of personality traits on patterns of emojis usage in Twitter (Li et al., 2018). To assess the users personality profiles, for each user, authors analyzed which words people use in tweets and found clear patterns of the emoji use specific to different personality traits. They found that people with high scores on neuroticism tend to use emojis to express exaggerated emotions. Extraverts and conscientious users use more positive than negative emojis. Finally, in general, emotionally unstable and agreeable people use more emojis overall.

Marengo et al. explored the relationship between personality and the use of emojis in a different way (Marengo et al., 2017). They presented participants with a set of 91 emojis and asked to self-identify with them. They found a positive correlation between the use of a blushing smiley and agreeableness, as well as that extraversion, is associated with positive emojis. Lastly, emojis with negative sentiment showed a negative correlation with emotional stability.

Finally, Völkel et al. studied the link between

user personality and emoji interpretation in context (Völkel et al., 2019). They measured the personality profile of people with the Big Five Inventory - a model that describes the emotional and behavioural tendencies of people in five dimensions (John and Srivastava, 1999). The model covers (1) Openness, related to willingness to try new things, (2) Conscientiousness - a tendency to show self-discipline, (3) Extraversion, which means the enjoyment from interaction with other people, (4) Agreeableness - valuing high getting along with others, and (5) Neuroticism - a tendency to feel and express negative emotions. Participants were shown a concrete message context and had to add an appropriate emoji to it. Then authors ran a generalized linear regression fitting BFI personality scores as predictors and counts of specific emojis as dependent variables. Authors claim that the choice of emojis is influenced by personality traits but do not point out specific links between personality traits and emojis using patterns.

In this work, I try to step back and explore the link between perception emoji and personality traits by analyzing how people with different personality profiles resolve ambiguity in emojis.

3 Methodology

3.1 Experiment

To test the impact of peoples BFI profile on the time they need to decide whether an emoji is suitable for the context or not, I conducted a reaction time experiment. The design was inspired by Jack Yates, who explored priming by dominance in ambiguous words by measuring reaction times participants needed to determine whether the presented word was ambiguous or not (Yates, 1978). Following his procedure, I presented participants with a short sentence followed by emoji and asked them to choose if the emoji was suitable for the context or not. For each sentence, I measured the time it took for the participants to make a decision. In the following subsections, I present a more detailed description of stimuli selection and experiment design.

3.2 Selection of the stimuli

There were 3633 emojis in the Unicode system by September 2021, when this work was started. I concentrated on emojis that represent either emotions or hand gestures since this study concentrates on the emotional expressiveness in communication and based on the claim that people with different personality types express and interpret emotions in different ways (Campbell and Rushton, 1978; Costa and McCrae, 1992). To make a set of ambiguous emojis stimuli, I assessed the Top 150 Twitter emojis in September 2021 [1] and chose those that fall into the Smileys People category. This resulted in a set of 74 emojis. Emojipedia [2] and Dictionary [3] provide interpretation and examples of the context of the use of emojis. For each emoji from my set, I looked through their pages on these sites and selected those for which at least two meanings were presented. As a result, I got a set of 23 emojis with several interpretations possible (Appendix 1). I used the renderings used in WhatsApp on the iOS operating system.

3.3 Context creation

For each emoji, I came up with two contexts, adapting those presented on the Emojipedia and Dictionary so that they are appropriate for the experiment. The goal of adaptation was to minimize the influence of the structure of the text on the reaction times. Hence all sentences were short (no more than 32 characters with a maximum variation of 2 words between sentences), affirmative, without punctuation and any professional terms, and in plain English (Appendix 1). For instance, I converted the example from Dictionary: *"This guy has been taking pics of his gf for like 30 minutes and hes being so patient with her omg so cute 🥺"* to *"This kitten is so cute 🥺"* so that the length of the sentence and slang language do not affect reading and reaction time. The contexts were treated as more or less equally probable, and none of them was treated as priming.

3.4 Experimental design

The experiment had the following procedure. The participants were given the task to read the sentence and answer the question of whether they think the emoji at the end of the sentence suits it or not. Each member rated a complete set of emojis. However, for counterbalancing purposes, the participants were randomly split into two groups and received emojis with different preceding contexts. In order to control the sequence effect, assuming that participants might experience fatigue or confusion after specific stimuli, the stimuli were presented

[1]https://emojitracker.com
[2]https://emojipedia.org
[3]https://www.dictionary.com

in random order. Stimuli appeared one after another, each on a separate page. To make a decision, participants had to select an option ("suitable"/" unsuitable") and then click the "Next" button. The experiment was conducted on the PsyToolkit platform (Stoet, 2010, 2017).

To make sure that the participants actually read the stimuli and did not just randomly select the answers, three filler questions were added, in the form of yes/no questions, asking about the content of the previous sentence.

3.5 Questionnaire

Participants' personality traits were assessed with the Big Five Inventory Questionnaire (John and Srivastava, 1999). I used the traditional full version of the inventory, consisting of 44 questions measuring (1) extraversion, (2) agreeableness, (3) conscientiousness, (4) neuroticism, and (5) openness. Participants had to choose to which extend the statements aimed to estimate different personality traits apply to them on a 7-point Likert scale.

In the end, I collected socio-demographic information about the participants, including gender, age, country of birth and residence, level of English proficiency. Also, I asked users to indicate from which device they took the survey.

3.6 Participants

I recruited participants from the same age group (18-27) and country of birth (Russia) to minimize the impact of these variables on outcome. The rationale behind such restrictions was that cultural factors could influence how people interpret emojis (Barbieri et al., 2016; Lu et al., 2016), and that people of different ages use emojis differently (Herring and Dainas, 2020; Koch et al., 2022). Moreover, participants were asked to indicate their level of English proficiency, and participants with language levels below intermediate were filtered out. Participants were recruited through the university mailing list and social media. One voucher for 1000 rubles was drawn among the participants.

I indicated the number of participants using the G*Power tool (Faul et al., 2007). An a priori analysis showed that I would need 138 participants if I hypothesize a large effect size of f2 = 0.15 and aim for statistical power of 0.95. I got 147 participants in total, 32 males and 115 females with a mean age of 24.

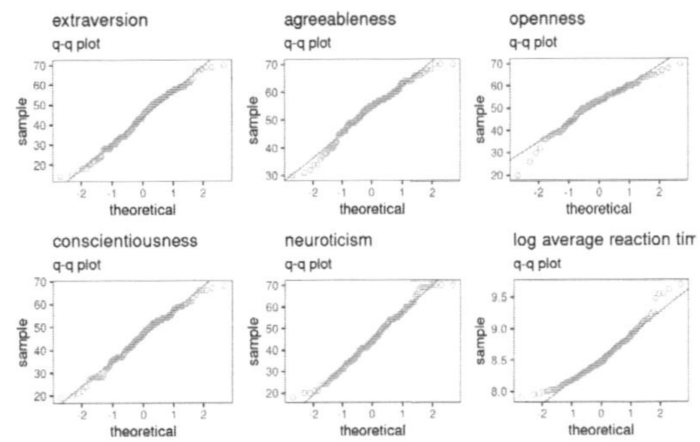

Figure 1: Quantile-Quantile plots for BFI scores and the logarithm of average reaction time.

3.7 Measures

The Reaction Time in the experiment was measured in milliseconds. For each participant, the average reaction time between all emojis was found. The average reaction time was not normally distributed, and I used its logarithm in further analysis. Two participants with outliers in reaction times were deleted from the sample.

For each personality trait from the BFI questionnaire, points for questions on the single construct were aggregated. Figure 1 shows the QQ-plots of personality traits and logarithmic average reaction times in my sample. For all BFI traits, I performed correlation analysis (Appendix 2). All correlations are below the level of 0.5, so I used all the variables in the analysis.

3.8 Model

I used the generalized linear regression models with an average reaction time as the dependent variable and BFI Traits and context as predictors (Stachl et al., 2017; Völkel et al., 2019). The study is exploratory, and I commuted several models. I ran separate models for each trait, adding the context as an interaction variable, and then made an aggregated model with all traits as predictors. I used the significance level of = 0.05. For the model comparison, I calculated R2, Adjusted R2, and Performance Score.

4 Results

In this section, I report the results of regression models (Makowski et al., 2021). I got statistically significant results for the (1) model predicting the reaction time with conscientiousness and context as an interaction, (2) model predicting the reaction time with neuroticism and context as an interaction, and (3) model with all BFI scores as predictors. The separate models with agreeableness, openness and extraversion and context as a predictor were statistically insignificant. In the following subsection, I describe the model performances in more detail. I provide the output of the models in Appendix 3.

4.1 Conscientiousness

The first model I fitted was a linear model (estimated using OLS) to predict the log of average reaction time with BFI conscientiousness score and context. The model explains a statistically significant and weak proportion of variance *($R2$ = 0.08, F(3, 135) = 3.93, p = 0.010, adj. $R2$ = 0.06).*

Within this model:
- The effect of conscientiousness is statistically significant and positive
- The effect of the context is statistically significant and positive
- The interaction effect of the context on conscientiousness is statistically significant and negative

Overall: from the model, we can see that the more conscientious the person is, the more time it takes for him to decide about the ambiguity of the emoji. However, in the case of this model, the context itself affects the reaction time more strongly and also has a negative interaction effect on conscientiousness.

4.2 Neuroticism

With a second model I predicted log of average reaction time with BFI neuroticism score and context. The model explains a statistically significant and weak proportion of variance *($R2$ = 0.08, F(3, 135) = 3.84, p = 0.011, adj. $R2$ = 0.06).*

Within this model:
- The effect of neuroticism is statistically significant and negative
- The effect of the context is statistically non-significant and negative
- The interaction effect of the context on neuroticism is statistically significant and positive

Overall: from this model, we can see that the more neurotic the person is, the more quickly he resolves the ambiguity in emoji, and the neuroticism is the most strong predictor in this model, but the context also plays a role as a positive interaction effect on the neuroticism.

4.3 Extraversion

The model predicting the log of average reaction time with BFI extraversion score and context was not statistically not significant and had a weak proportion of variance *($R2$ = 0.03, F(3, 135) = 1.23, p = 0.302, adj. $R2$ = 4.93e-03).*

Within this model:
- The effect of extraversion is statistically non-significant and positive
- The effect of the context is statistically non-significant and positive
- The interaction effect of the context on extraversion is statistically non-significant and negative

Overall: even though the model is not significant, we still can see a tiny trend that more extraversive people might resolve ambiguity slower. However, the model performance does not allow us to make such conclusions.

4.4 Openness

The model predicting the log of average reaction time with BFI openness score and context was not statistically not significant and had a weak proportion of variance *($R2$ = 0.03, F(3, 135) = 1.42, p = 0.240, adj. $R2$ = 9.06e-03).*

Within this model:
- The effect of openness is statistically non-significant and negative
- The effect of the context is statistically non-significant and negative
- The interaction effect of the context on openness is statistically non-significant and positive

Overall: although this model is also insignificant, we can see a little trend with more open people needing more time to decide about ambiguous emoji, but the model has the too poor performance to draw any conclusions.

4.5 Agreeableness

The last model with a single BFI predictor was the model predicting the log of average reaction time with BFI agreeableness score and context. The model explains a statistically not significant and weak proportion of variance *($R2$ = 0.03, F(3, 135) = 1.16, p = 0.327, adj. $R2$ = 3.50e-03).*

Within this model:

- The effect of agreeableness is statistically non-significant and positive
- The effect of the context is statistically non-significant and positive
- The interaction effect of the context on agreeableness is statistically non-significant and negative

Overall: the model is not significant, though, the trend we can see in it is that the more agreeable the person is, the less time it might take for him to resolve the ambiguity in emoji, but the model is not significant to claim that.

4.6 All traits

Finally, I fitted a linear model to predict the log of average reaction time with openness, conscientiousness, neuroticism, agreeableness, extraversion and context. The model explains a statistically significant and moderate proportion of variance *(R2 = 0.14, F(10, 128) = 2.02, p = 0.037, adj. R2 = 0.07)*.

Within this model:
- The effect of openness is statistically non-significant and negative
- The effect of conscientiousness is statistically significant and positive
- The effect of neuroticism is statistically non-significant and negative
- The effect of agreeableness is statistically non-significant and negative
- The effect of extraversion is statistically non-significant and negative
- The effect of the context is statistically non-significant and negative
- The interaction effect of the context on openness is statistically non-significant and positive
- The interaction effect of the context on conscientiousness is statistically significant and negative
- The interaction effect of the context on neuroticism is statistically non-significant and positive
- The interaction effect of the context on agreeableness is statistically non-significant and positive

Overall: out of this model, we can see that with an increase in conscientiousness score, it takes more time for the person to resolve the ambiguity. On the contrary, the higher score in neuroticism decreases the time it takes for the person to decide about the ambiguous emoji. The strongest predictor in the model is the interaction between the context and conscientiousness, assuming that the effect of conscientiousness on reaction time also depends on the context in which the person sees the emoji.

For all the models, the standardized parameters were obtained by fitting the model on a standardized version of the dataset.

4.7 Best model

Having all the models together, I compared the statistically significant models between each other to identify the best one with the performance R package (Lüdecke et al., 2021). The result is reported in Table 1. Looking at the performance score and adjusted R-squared, we can see that the most powerful one is the model with all BFI personality traits and context as an interaction as predictors.

5 Limitations and Discussion

I ran an experiment to explore whether there is a link between how people perceive ambiguous emojis and their personality traits. With the regression analysis, I found that the scores on conscientiousness and neuroticism serve as significant predictors of how much time does it take for a person to resolve the ambiguity in emoji, with more conscientious people needing more time and more neurotic people needing less time to decide about an ambiguous emoji. For both significant variables, the interaction effect of the context was also significant. Openness, agreeableness and extraversion did not show any significant effect on the reaction time.

These results are in line with previous research. Lots of studies demonstrated that people scoring high on neuroticism, even though performing poor on the complex and stressful tasks, show high performance on simple and repeated tasks (Corr, 2003; Oswald et al., 2017; Poposki et al., 2009; Studer-Luethi et al., 2012). In turn, conscientious people tend to overestimate the importance of tasks, which makes their learning times and decision-making slower (Lepine et al., 2006; Martocchio and Judge, 1997; Murray et al., 2014; Studer-Luethi et al., 2012). The importance of context variables as an interaction also supports previous research claiming the importance of semantics for emoji interpretation (Miller et al., 2016, 2017; Tigwell and Flatla, 2016; Völkel et al., 2019).

Considering previous research, I might interpret my results in a way that conscientious people being achievement striving, careful and not impulsive

Name	R2	R2 (adj.)	AIC_wt	BIC_wt	Performance
all predictors	0.1360748	0.0685807	0.0360656	0.0000013	0.6666667
conscientiousness	0.0803673	0.0599310	0.5140960	0.5333301	0.4010676
neuroticism	0.0785988	0.0581233	0.4498385	0.4666686	0.2900979

Table 1: Comparison of statistically significant models

tend to solve any tasks more responsively, read the context carefully and need more time to decide about the meaning of the emoji. Neurotic people being anxious and impulsive, might make their decisions in a less analytic and more emotional and spontaneous way. What is more, trying to minimize the effect of culture on the results, I recruited participants from the same country of origin. However, having that context as an important interaction variable might mean that, first, the semantic wrapping is important in interpreting emoji, but also that people from same countries have similar information resources and patterns of communication. Therefore, one of the contexts might be more intuitive and familiar to them.

The study has several limitations. First, my sample was biased towards females, and since the related work has found that gender can influence the interpretation of the emojis (Chen et al., 2018; Herring and Dainas, 2020; Koch et al., 2022), the analysis might benefit from a more balanced data. Moreover, I did not restrict the users to use the same operational systems, and even though I controlled the renderings of emojis on the experimental platform, people who usually use different operating systems and use different renderings might have some confusion seeing the appearance of emojis to which they are not used to. Finally, to deal with the sequence effects, I showed the emojis randomly, and due to the limitations of the PsyToolkit platform, I was not able to make a Latin Square Counterbalancing remembering the order of emoji for each of the participants. It would be nice to see whether some possibly confusing emoji affect the reaction time needed to decide about the following one.

In this research, I concentrated only on participants' reaction times. Future work might benefit from adding their answers about whether they found the emoji suitable or not. What is more, only by-subject analysis is performed in this study. I performed an exploratory analysis by-item and found noticeably high average reaction times for the following emojis 🙌, 🤭, 😳. Future work will include by-item analysis and explore the difference in reaction times between people with different personalities for each of the emojis, fitting a separate regression model for all of them.

Considering implications, nowadays, smartphones and laptops have become an integral part of our lives, and interactive computer systems are becoming more adaptive, tracking our behaviour and modelling search results based on it, suggesting words and stickers. With a knowledge of how people with different personality traits interpret emojis in different systems and applications can improve the user experience. For example, it is possible to communicate ambiguity by using ambiguous emojis in correspondence between people with different personality profiles, thereby reducing miscommunication. For instance, highlighting emojis, which other person tend to use with different contexts, or suggesting alternative less ambiguous emojis. What is more, the user's personality can be taken to account in the automatic reply systems and chatbots.

6 Conclusion

Because of the spread of text communication methods, emojis became popular, and serve as a kind of replacement for non-verbal emotional cues. This should make the text less ambiguous and eliminate miscommunication. However, different people may interpret emojis in different ways. Few studies explored the relationship between personality and how people perceive emojis. However, most of the existing research concentrates on emojis out of context, while they are usually used as an addition to text. In this paper, I tried to address this gap and investigated how users with different personality traits perceive emoji ambiguity in context. I found that conscientiousness increases the time it takes a person to resolve an emoji ambiguity. On the contrary, people with a high level of neuroticism make decisions about the interpretation of emojis faster. The context turned out to be a significant interaction effect. Thus, it can be concluded that personality traits have a relationship with how users perceive and interpret emojis. These findings can be used in the design of responsive, interactive systems, make their use more personalized and reduce miscommunication in text messaging.

Acknowledgements

I thank Patrizia Paggio for her valuable advice and feedback.

References

Paul M. Aoki and Allison Woodruff. 2005. Making space for stories: Ambiguity in the design of personal communication systems. In *Proceedings of the SIGCHI Conference on Human Factors in Computing Systems*, CHI '05, page 181190, New York, NY, USA. Association for Computing Machinery.

Francesco Barbieri, German Kruszewski, Francesco Ronzano, and Horacio Saggion. 2016. How cosmopolitan are emojis? exploring emojis usage and meaning over different languages with distributional semantics. In *Proceedings of the 24th ACM International Conference on Multimedia*, MM '16, page 531535, New York, NY, USA. Association for Computing Machinery.

Janet Beavin Bavelas and Nicole Chovil. 2000. Visible acts of meaning: An integrated message model of language in face-to-face dialogue. *Journal of Language and Social Psychology*, 19(2):163–194.

Barend Beekhuizen, Blair C. Armstrong, and Suzanne Stevenson. 2021. Probing lexical ambiguity: Word vectors encode number and relatedness of senses. *Cognitive science*, 45 5:e12943.

J.K. Burgoon, L.K. Guerrero, and K. Floyd. 2010. *Nonverbal Communication*. MySearchLab Series 15% Off Series. Allyn & Bacon.

Anne Campbell and J. P. Rushton. 1978. Bodily communication and personality. *The British journal of social and clinical psychology*, 17 1:31–6.

Zhenpeng Chen, Xuan Lu, Wei Ai, Huoran Li, Qiaozhu Mei, and Xuanzhe Liu. 2018. Through a gender lens: Learning usage patterns of emojis from large-scale android users. In *Proceedings of the 2018 World Wide Web Conference*, WWW '18, page 763772, Republic and Canton of Geneva, CHE. International World Wide Web Conferences Steering Committee.

Philip J. Corr. 2003. Personality and dual-task processing: disruption of procedural learning by declarative processing. *Personality and Individual Differences*, 34(7):1245–1269.

Paul T. Costa and Robert R. McCrae. 1980. Influence of extraversion and neuroticism on subjective well-being: happy and unhappy people. *Journal of personality and social psychology*, 38 4:668–78.

Paul T. Costa and Robert R. McCrae. 1992. Four ways five factors are basic. *Personality and Individual Differences*, 13(6):653–665.

Henriette Cramer, Paloma de Juan, and Joel Tetreault. 2016. Sender-intended functions of emojis in us messaging. In *Proceedings of the 18th International Conference on Human-Computer Interaction with Mobile Devices and Services*, MobileHCI '16, page 504509, New York, NY, USA. Association for Computing Machinery.

João Cunha, Nuno Lourenço, Pedro Martins, and Penousal Machado. 2020. Visual blending for concept representation: A case study on emoji generation. *New Generation Computing*, 38.

Marc Davis and Ned Holbrook. Unicode emoji.

Daantje Derks, Agneta Fischer, and Arjan Bos. 2008. The role of emotion in computer-mediated communication: A review. *Computers in Human Behavior*, 24:766–785.

Franz Faul, Edgar Erdfelder, Albert-Georg Lang, and Axel Buchner. 2007. G*power 3: A flexible statistical power analysis program for the social, behavioral, and biomedical sciences. *Behavior Research Methods*, 39:175–191.

Susan C. Herring and Ashley R. Dainas. 2020. Gender and age influences on interpretation of emoji functions. *Trans. Soc. Comput.*, 3(2).

Tianran Hu, Han Guo, Hao Sun, Thuy-vy Thi Nguyen, and Jiebo Luo. 2017. Spice up your chat: The intentions and sentiment effects of using emoji.

Sara Jaeger, Yixun Xia, Pui-Yee Lee, Denise Hunter, Michelle Beresford, and Gastón Ares. 2017. Emoji questionnaires can be used with a range of population segments: Findings relating to age, gender and frequency of emoji/emoticon use. *Food Quality and Preference*, 68.

Oliver P. John and Sanjay Srivastava. 1999. The big five trait taxonomy: History, measurement, and theoretical perspectives.

Linda K. Kaye, Helen J. Wall, and Stephanie A. Malone. 2016. turn that frown upside-down: A contextual account of emoticon usage on different virtual platforms. *Computers in Human Behavior*, 60:463–467.

Ryan Kelly and Leon Watts. 2015. Characterising the inventive appropriation of emoji as relationally meaningful in mediated close personal relationships. Experiences of Technology Appropriation: Unanticipated Users, Usage, Circumstances, and Design ; Conference date: 20-09-2015 Through 20-09-2015.

Timo K. Koch, Peter Romero, and Clemens Stachl. 2022. Age and gender in language, emoji, and emoticon usage in instant messages. *Computers in Human Behavior*, 126:106990.

Petra Kralj Novak, Jasmina Smailovi, Borut Sluban, and Igor Mozeti. 2015. Sentiment of emojis. *PLOS ONE*, 10(12):1–22.

Robert Lengel and Richard Daft. 1984. An exploratory analysis of the relationship between media richness and managerial information processing. page 73.

Jeffrey Lepine, Jason Colquitt, and Amir Erez. 2006. Adaptability to changing task contexts: Effects of general cognitive ability conscientiousness, and openness to experience. *Personnel Psychology*, 53:563 – 593.

Weijian Li, Yuxiao Chen, Tianran Hu, and Jiebo Luo. 2018. Mining the relationship between emoji usage patterns and personality.

Shao-Kang Lo. 2008. The nonverbal communication functions of emoticons in computer-mediated communication. *Cyberpsychology behavior : the impact of the Internet, multimedia and virtual reality on behavior and society*, 11:595–7.

Xuan Lu, Wei Ai, Xuanzhe Liu, Qian Li, Ning Wang, Gang Huang, and Qiaozhu Mei. 2016. Learning from the ubiquitous language: An empirical analysis of emoji usage of smartphone users. In *Proceedings of the 2016 ACM International Joint Conference on Pervasive and Ubiquitous Computing*, UbiComp '16, page 770780, New York, NY, USA. Association for Computing Machinery.

Daniel Lüdecke, Mattan S. Ben-Shachar, Indrajeet Patil, Philip Waggoner, and Dominique Makowski. 2021. performance: An r package for assessment, comparison and testing of statistical models. *Journal of Open Source Software*, 6(60):3139.

Dominique Makowski, Mattan S. Ben-Shachar, Indrajeet Patil, and Daniel Lüdecke. 2021. Automated results reporting as a practical tool to improve reproducibility and methodological best practices adoption. *CRAN*.

Davide Marengo, Fabrizia Giannotta, and Michele Settanni. 2017. Assessing personality using emoji: An exploratory study. *Personality and Individual Differences*, 112:74–78.

Joseph J. Martocchio and Timothy A. Judge. 1997. Relationship between conscientiousness and learning in employee training: mediating influences of self-deception and self-efficacy. *The Journal of applied psychology*, 82 5:764–73.

Hannah Miller, Daniel Kluver, Jacob Thebault-Spieker, Loren Terveen, and Brent Hecht. 2017. Understanding emoji ambiguity in context: The role of text in emoji-related miscommunication. *Proceedings of the International AAAI Conference on Web and Social Media*, 11(1):152–161.

Hannah Miller, Jacob Thebault-Spieker, Shuo Chang, Isaac Johnson, Loren Terveen, and Brent Hecht. 2016. "blissfully happy" or "ready to fight": Varying interpretations of emoji.

Aja L. Murray, Wendy Johnson, Matt McGue, and William G. Iacono. 2014. How are conscientiousness and cognitive ability related to one another? a re-examination of the intelligence compensation hypothesis. *Personality and Individual Differences*, 70:17–22.

Frederick Oswald, Zach Hambrick, and L. Jones. 2017. *Keeping All the Plates Spinning: Understanding and Predicting Multitasking Performance*, pages 77–96.

Umashanthi Pavalanathan and Jacob Eisenstein. 2015. Emoticons vs. emojis on twitter: A causal inference approach.

Elizabeth Poposki, Frederick Oswald, and Hubert Chen. 2009. Neuroticism negatively affects multitasking performance through state anxiety. page 29.

Marília Prada, David Rodrigues, Rita Silva, and Margarida Garrido. 2016. Lisbon symbol database (lsd): Subjective norms for 600 symbols. *Behavior research methods*, 48.

Marília Prada, David L. Rodrigues, Margarida V. Garrido, Diniz Lopes, Bernardo Cavalheiro, and Rui Gaspar. 2018. Motives, frequency and attitudes toward emoji and emoticon use. *Telematics and Informatics*, 35(7):1925–1934.

David Rodrigues, Diniz Lopes, Marília Prada, Dominic Thompson, and Margarida V. Garrido. 2017. A frown emoji can be worth a thousand words: Perceptions of emoji use in text messages exchanged between romantic partners. *Telematics and Informatics*, 34(8):1532–1543.

Clemens Stachl, Sven Hilbert, Quay Au, Daniel Buschek, Alexander De Luca, Bernd Bischl, Heinrich Hussmann, and Markus Buehner. 2017. Personality traits predict smartphone usage. *European Journal of Personality*, 31.

Barbara Studer-Luethi, Susanne M. Jaeggi, Martin Buschkuehl, and Walter J. Perrig. 2012. Influence of neuroticism and conscientiousness on working memory training outcome. *Personality and Individual Differences*, 53(1):44–49.

Garreth W. Tigwell and David R. Flatla. 2016. Oh that's what you meant! reducing emoji misunderstanding. MobileHCI '16, page 859866, New York, NY, USA. Association for Computing Machinery.

Sarah Theres Völkel, Daniel Buschek, Jelena Pranjic, and Heinrich Hussmann. 2019. Understanding emoji interpretation through user personality and message context. In *Proceedings of the 21st International Conference on Human-Computer Interaction with Mobile Devices and Services*, MobileHCI '19, New York, NY, USA. Association for Computing Machinery.

Joseph Walther. 2011. Theories of computer-mediated communication and interpersonal relations. *The Handbook of Interpersonal Communication*, pages 443–479.

Sanjaya Wijeratne, Lakshika Balasuriya, Amit Sheth, and Derek Doran. 2016. Emojinet: Building a machine readable sense inventory for emoji. volume 10046.

Sanjaya Wijeratne, Lakshika Balasuriya, Amit Sheth, and Derek Doran. 2017. Emojinet: An open service and api for emoji sense discovery.

Alecia Wolf. 2000. Emotional expression online: Gender differences in emoticon use. *CyberPsychology Behavior*, 3.

Jack Yates. 1978. Priming dominant and unusual senses of ambiguous words. *Memory & Cognition*, 6:636–643.

Hyejin Youn, Logan Sutton, Eric Smith, Cristopher Moore, Jon F. Wilkins, Ian Maddieson, William Croft, and Tanmoy Bhattacharya. 2016. On the universal structure of human lexical semantics. *Proceedings of the National Academy of Sciences*, 113(7):1766–1771.

A Appendix

A.1 Appendix 1: Final set of emoji with context

Context 1	Context 2
Please get well soon 🙏	We won this round 🙏
Huge discounts on friday 😱	Couldn't sleep after the movie 😱
Cant even think about exam 😬	I spilled coffee near professor 😬
Let's pretend we didn't see it 🙈	She gave me such a nice gift 🙈
This kitten is so cute 🥺	That's such sad news 🥺
Some sharks live to 500 years 😳	Sent her a selfie instead of docs 😳
They have no tickets left 🤷‍♂️	No idea what gift to buy 🤷‍♂️
I'm tired and ready for bed 🥱	Falling asleep in class 🥱
I am really exhausted 😪	Kitten is back at the shelter 😪
Dont know what do you mean 👀	Look at that woman over there 👀
I don't know as I was not there 👐	I miss and can't wait to see you 👐
I heard about your exam! 👏	Everything is closed again 👏
His arrogance must be stopped 👊	You did a very brave thing 👊
Nice to meet you ✋	Very good thought ✋
I dont care actually 💁‍♀️	That's what it means 💁‍♀️
Its extremely hot today 😩	I am so tired of all this work 😩
So tired of my allergies 🤧	I've just watched Hatiko 🤧
I cannot believe it is true 😵	Looks like I drank too much 😵
Thats mind-blowing 💥	What a great news 💥
I finally received my degree 😎	What a good weather today 😎
No idea on what do you mean 🙄	Need some help to carry the sofa 🙄
She yelled at her husband 🤭	This dirt is disgusting 🤭

A.2 Appendix 2: Correlation plot for BFI scores

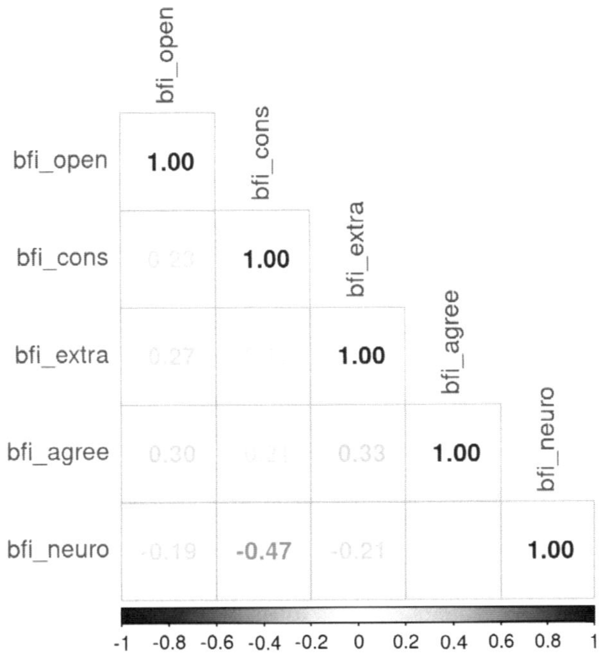

A.3 Appendix 3: Regression models' outputs

Conscientiousness and context

	Model 1
(Intercept)	7.99***
	(0.18)
bfi_cons	0.01**
	(0.00)
group2	0.78**
	(0.26)
bfi_cons:group2	−0.01**
	(0.01)
R^2	0.08
Adj. R^2	0.06
Num. obs.	139

$^{***}p < 0.001$; $^{**}p < 0.01$; $^{*}p < 0.05$

Table 2: Conscientiousness and context

Neuroticism and context

	Model 1
(Intercept)	8.89***
	(0.15)
bfi_neuro	−0.01**
	(0.00)
group2	−0.36
	(0.22)
bfi_neuro:group2	0.01*
	(0.00)
R^2	0.08
Adj. R^2	0.06
Num. obs.	139

$^{***}p < 0.001$; $^{**}p < 0.01$; $^{*}p < 0.05$

Table 3: Neuroticism and context

Extraversion and context

	Model 1
(Intercept)	8.48^{***}
	(0.15)
bfi_extra	0.00
	(0.00)
group2	0.25
	(0.22)
bfi_extra:group2	-0.00
	(0.00)
R^2	0.03
Adj. R^2	0.00
Num. obs.	139

$^{***}p < 0.001$; $^{**}p < 0.01$; $^{*}p < 0.05$

Table 4: Extraversion and context

Agreeableness and context

	Model 1
(Intercept)	8.57^{***}
	(0.28)
bfi_agree	-0.00
	(0.01)
group2	0.21
	(0.39)
bfi_agree:group2	-0.00
	(0.01)
R^2	0.03
Adj. R^2	0.00
Num. obs.	139

$^{***}p < 0.001$; $^{**}p < 0.01$; $^{*}p < 0.05$

Table 5: Agreeableness and context

Openness and context

	Model 1
(Intercept)	8.45^{***}
	(0.26)
bfi_open	0.00
	(0.00)
group2	−0.19
	(0.39)
bfi_open:group2	0.01
	(0.01)
R^2	0.03
Adj. R^2	0.01
Num. obs.	139

$^{***}p < 0.001$; $^{**}p < 0.01$; $^{*}p < 0.05$

Table 6: Statistical models

All BFI traits scores and context

	Model 1
(Intercept)	8.73^{***}
	(0.41)
bfi_open	0.00
	(0.01)
bfi_cons	0.01
	(0.00)
bfi_neuro	−0.01
	(0.00)
bfi_agree	−0.01
	(0.01)
bfi_extra	−0.00
	(0.00)
group2	−0.12
	(0.63)
bfi_open:group2	0.01
	(0.01)
bfi_cons:group2	-0.01^{*}
	(0.01)
bfi_neuro:group2	0.01
	(0.01)
bfi_agree:group2	0.00
	(0.01)
R^2	0.14
Adj. R^2	0.07
Num. obs.	139

$^{***}p < 0.001$; $^{**}p < 0.01$; $^{*}p < 0.05$

Table 7: All BFI traits scores and context

Semantic Congruency Facilitates Memory for Emojis

Andriana L. Christofalos and **Laurie Beth Feldman** and **Heather Sheridan**
University at Albany, State University of New York, Albany, NY, USA
{achristofalos,lfeldman,hsheridan}@albany.edu

Abstract

Emojis can assume different relations with the sentence context in which they occur. While affective elaboration and emoji-word redundancy are frequently investigated in laboratory experiments, the role of emojis in inferential processes has received much less attention. Here, we used an online ratings task and a recognition memory task to investigate whether differences in emoji function within a sentence affect judgments of emoji-text coherence and subsequent recognition accuracy. Emojis that function as synonyms of a target word from the passages were rated as better fitting with the passage (more coherent) than emojis consistent with an inference from the passage, and both types of emojis were rated as more coherent than incongruent (unrelated) emojis. In a recognition test, emojis consistent with the semantic content of passages (synonym and inference emojis) were better recognized than incongruent emojis. Findings of the present study provide corroborating evidence that readers extract semantic information from emojis and then integrate it with surrounding passage content.

1 Emojis and Word Processing

Recent research using both ratings tasks and online processing measures has shown that emojis that are redundant (i.e., synonymous) with a target word can facilitate text comprehension (Daniel and Camp, 2020). Barach and colleagues (Barach et al., 2021) used eye tracking measures to examine how readers benefit from the presence of non-face emojis that were positioned at the end of sentences and were synonymous with the target word (e.g., coffee). They compared sentences with emojis that were either semantically congruent with the target word (e.g., "My tall coffee is just the right temperature "), semantically incongruent (e.g., "My tall coffee is just the right temperature "), and sentences without an emoji ("My tall coffee is just the right temperature"). Participants in their experiment read the sentences for comprehension while their eye movements were recorded. The congruent emojis were skipped more often and fixated for less time than the incongruent emojis, and the overall sentence reading times were shorter when the emojis were congruent compared to incongruent with the proceeding text. These effects of semantic congruency reported by Barach and colleagues (Barach et al., 2021) suggest that, similar to semantic congruency effects with words, readers extract semantic information from emojis and integrate it with the surrounding text. Similar findings were shown when text includes face emojis, which can convey more subtle and less literal meanings than non-face emojis (Beyersmann et al., 2022), and when emojis were used to replace words in sentences (Cohn et al., 2018; Scheffler et al., 2022; Weissman, 2019).

2 Emojis and Higher-Level Language Processing

In contrast to the research summarized above that examined linguistic processing of emojis associated with the meaning of isolated words, other studies have examined how readers process sentences with emojis that cannot be mapped to a single word, such as the detection of sarcastic intent (Garcia et al., 2022; Weissman and Tanner, 2018) and other types of indirect messages that go beyond the literal meaning of a statement (Holtgraves and Robinson, 2020).

Both behavioral and neurophysiological measures indicate that a winking face emoji invites sarcastic and ironic interpretations during reading (Garcia et al., 2022; Weissman and Tanner, 2018). For example, accuracy in detecting sarcastic intent increased when a winking face emoji was present, demonstrating that the presence of an emoji can promote sarcastic relative to more literal sentence interpretations (Garcia et al., 2022).

Proceedings of the The Fifth International Workshop on Emoji Understanding and Applications in Social Media, pages 63 - 68
July 14, 2022 ©2022 Association for Computational Linguistics

In addition to sarcasm, the presence of an emoji can disambiguate other indirect aspects of sentence meaning. Holtgraves and Robinson (Holtgraves and Robinson, 2020) had participants read a series of questions followed by indirect replies that either contained an emoji (e.g., a worried face) or did not contain an emoji. For disclosures (e.g., "How did you do in chemistry?") and opinions (e.g., "What did you think of my presentation?"), but not requests for actions (e.g., "Can you type my term paper for me?"), judgements about whether a reply was congruent with the intent of the question were more accurate and faster when the reply contained an emoji than when it did not. Collectively, these findings provide evidence that emojis can help to offset a discrepancy between literal and nonliteral aspects of meaning, often associated with grasping a speaker's intent.

3 Memory for Emojis in Text

In contrast to the comprehension effects delineated above, only two studies have examined effects of emojis on memory (Chatzichristos et al., 2020; Homann et al., 2022). Chatzichristos and colleagues (Chatzichristos et al., 2020) provided evidence that emojis can influence memory for autobiographical events during reading. Participants in this study completed a retrieval task for autobiographic memories cued by a word paired either with a positive or a negative face emoji. Emotional incongruity of word-emoji pairs led to longer reaction times for retrieval as well as enhanced activation in brain areas associated with language-induced semantic conflict, suggesting that emoji affect influenced memory retrieval.

To examine how memory for emojis differs from memory for words, Homann and colleagues (Homann et al., 2022) compared isolated words or emojis under full attention and under divided attention conditions. In the divided attention condition, participants recalled the previously studied stimuli while completing a distractor 1-back recall task with one of three types of materials (i.e., words, emojis, and shapes). In that study, recall performance was better for isolated emojis than for words. In addition, recall memory for words was more disrupted when the simultaneous distractor task involved words, whereas declines in recall accuracy were smaller when the distractor task involved emojis. However, emoji recall was equally good when a distractor task involved emojis, words, or shapes. The authors concluded that because emojis have not only verbal but also distinctive visuo-spatial attributes, they interfere less with memory for single words and for each other than do words. The findings by (Chatzichristos et al., 2020) suggest that emojis impact memory retrieval, and the findings by (Homann et al., 2022) suggest that the combination of both verbal and visuo-spatial attributes of emojis makes them easier to recall in memory than words.

The levels of processing framework proposes that semantic elaboration results in stronger memory traces than shallower processing (Craik and Lockhart, 1972), therefore, memory can be enhanced for content that is semantically congruent with surrounding context (e.g., (Packard et al., 2017)). The classic finding is that when participants are instructed to process single words for form (shallow processing) as compared with for meaning (deep processing), encoding for deep level processing takes longer but, importantly, recall accuracy is higher (Craik and Tulving, 1975). Typically, comparisons of processing depth for recognition memory have been demonstrated for single words (Craik and Tulving, 1975). Researchers have yet to examine memory for emojis whose integration with text requires different degrees of semantic processing.

Central to the present study, we understand inferential processing to entail a deeper level of semantic analysis than the semantic processing of isolated words (Mason and Just, 2004) and we ask whether memory can be modulated by emoji-induced elaborations on critical regions of a sentence (Sanford et al., 2006). Precisely aligned stress on critical words in speech (Fraundorf et al., 2010), or italicizing or bolding in text (Sanford et al., 2006), can signal focus. Here we assume that emojis can provide a similar marker of focus and we ask whether memory for emojis may differ depending on whether the emoji-text relation supports shallower (word substitution) or deeper (inference) processing.

4 Present Study

Whereas prior work has often focused on the impact of substituting a word for an emoji, the current study instead presents the text and emoji at the same time to explore how readers integrate emojis with the preceding context. The present study examined emoji-text coherence and recognition memory for emojis whose function supports either a

Emoji Condition	Passage
Congruent Inference	Bobby brought home a new pet to live in the tank. He hoped he would remember to buy some mice to feed it on his way home from basketball practice the next night. 🐍
Congruent Synonym	Bobby brought home a new pet to live in the tank. He hoped he would remember to buy some mice to feed it on his way home from basketball practice the next night. 🏀
Incongruent	Bobby brought home a new pet to live in the tank. He hoped he would remember to buy some mice to feed it on his way home from basketball practice the next night. ⚖️

Table 1: Sample stimuli. The target word in this example is underlined.

lower- or higher-level analysis of passage meaning. We predicted that emojis consistent with passage content (congruent synonym and congruent inference emojis) would have higher coherence as measured by fit ratings than the emojis we selected to be irrelevant to the passages (incongruent emojis). Based on the levels of processing framework and prior work showing that readers show semantic congruency effects for emojis during reading (Barach et al., 2021; Beyersmann et al., 2022), we predicted that readers would show higher recognition accuracy for emojis that are congruent with the surrounding passage content (synonym and inference emojis) than incongruent emojis. Extrapolating from the levels of processing framework (Craik and Lockhart, 1972), we also hypothesized a memory advantage for emojis consistent with passage inferences, such that readers would show higher recognition accuracy for inference emojis than for synonym emojis.

4.1 Participants

Participants consisted of 89 undergraduate students at a large university in the northeast United States who completed the study for course credit.

4.2 Materials

Sixty short passages were created for the present study. Some passages were modified from materials of (Virtue and Motyka Joss, 2017). All passages consisted of two sentences and an emoji. Both sentences contained cues to an inference, and the second sentence included an elaboration about a target word. Each passage was paired with three non-emotion, object emojis: 1) an emoji consistent with the inference (congruent inference), 2) an emoji consistent with the meaning of a target word within the passage (congruent synonym), and 3) an emoji that was irrelevant to the passage (incongruent). Emojis were always positioned at the end of the passage, and no emoji appeared in more than one sentence context. See Table 1 for sample stimuli.

4.3 Procedure

Participants completed one of six counterbalanced versions of an online Qualtrics survey with two parts (rating, recognition). Versions were counterbalanced on emoji condition (congruent synonym, congruent inference, incongruent) in the ratings task, and on whether the emoji item was old or new in the subsequent recognition task. For each participant, ten passages were paired with a congruent synonym emoji, a different ten passages were paired with a congruent inference emoji, and a third set of ten passages was paired with an incongruent emoji. Participants first completed a ratings task in which they were shown 30 passages with an emoji. One passage was displayed per page, and for each passage, participants rated how well the emoji fits with the passage by choosing among five choices, "Not well at all", "Slightly well", "Moderately well", "Very well", "Extremely well". After the emoji ratings task, participants completed a demographics questionnaire. Then, participants completed a recognition memory task with 60 emojis, half of which had appeared in the rating task. For each trial in the recognition task, participants were shown an emoji and were asked to make an old/new judgment, to indicate whether they had seen the emoji paired with a passage in the rating task (i.e., old) or if the emoji had not been previously presented (i.e., new).

5 Results

Data from 23 participants who had low recognition accuracy (i.e., below 60% accuracy) were removed from the dataset. After removal, the dataset consists of data from 66 participants.

5.1 Emoji-Text Coherence

A linear mixed-effect model was performed using the lme4 package in R (Bates et al., 2015) to examine emoji-text coherence ratings between the three emoji conditions. Measures of emoji-text coherence were based on participants' judgments of emoji fit with the accompanying passage based on a five-point scale, and fit judgments were converted to numeric ratings (5 = high coherence). Mean coherence ratings differed as a function of the relation of the emoji to passage (emoji condition), $F(2, 1866.5) = 921.45$, $p < .001$. Pairwise comparisons showed that participants provided higher coherence ratings for congruent inference emojis than incongruent emojis ($t(1876) = 32.45$, $p < .001$, $d = 1.67$), and higher coherence ratings for congruent synonym emojis than incongruent emojis ($t(1869) = 40.56$, $p < .001$, $d = 2.25$). Finally, participants judged congruent synonym emojis to be more coherent than congruent inference emojis ($t(1869) = -8.09$, $p < .001$, $d = .35$). Table 2 summarizes emoji-text coherence based on mean ratings of fit and standard error for each emoji condition.

5.2 Emoji Recognition Accuracy

A logistic mixed-effect model was performed using the lme4 package in R (Bates et al., 2015) to examine the effect of emoji condition on recognition accuracy for emojis that had been previously presented in passages for coherence judgments. Mean recognition accuracy significantly differed as a function of emoji condition, ($\chi^2 = 15.90$, $p < .001$). Pairwise comparisons showed that participants had higher recognition accuracy for inference emojis compared to incongruent emojis ($z = 3.88$, $p <.001$, $d = .23$) and participants had higher recognition accuracy for synonym emojis compared to incongruent emojis ($z = 2.41$, $p = .02$, $d = .11$). Recognition accuracy was numerically, but not significantly, higher for inference emojis compared to synonym emojis ($z = 1.71$, $p =.09$, $d = .12$). Table 2 shows mean recognition accuracy (i.e., proportion correct for old emoji items) and standard error for each emoji condition.

Emoji Condition	Emoji-Text Coherence (Fit Ratings)	Recognition Accuracy (Proportion Correct)
Congruent Inference	3.12 (.05)	.90 (.01)
Congruent Synonym	3.56 (.05)	.86 (.01)
Incongruent	1.30 (.03)	.82 (.01)

Table 2: Mean emoji-text coherence ratings and mean recognition accuracy for old emojis. Standard error in parentheses.

6 Discussion

The goal of the present study was to examine emoji-text coherence and recognition memory for emojis that appear in passage-final position and relate to passages in one of three ways. With respect to judgments of coherence, readers judged congruent emojis (synonym and inference emojis) as better fitting with the passages than incongruent emojis. In addition, readers judged synonym emojis as better fitting with the passages than inference emojis.

With respect to recognition accuracy, results show that, consistent with the levels of processing framework, readers had more accurate recognition memory for emojis that were semantically relevant to the paired text compared to emojis that were not related to the text, suggesting that readers encoded the semantic content of the emojis and integrated it with the surrounding text. The present study extends previous findings suggesting that readers show semantic congruency effects in online processing measures (Barach et al., 2021; Beyersmann et al., 2022) by providing insight about what is retained in memory shortly after reading passages with emojis. Specifically, our findings suggest that readers encode the semantic properties of emojis in memory and show better recognition of semantically congruent emojis compared to semantically-incongruent emojis after a short delay. Contrary to the degree of semantic elaboration within the levels of processing framework (Craik and Lockhart, 1972), readers showed a numerical, but not a statistically reliable benefit for inference emojis compared to synonym emojis.

6.1 Limitations

The decision to place emojis in passage final position was based on two factors: 1) the evidence that integration processes occur late in comprehension (Kintsch, 1988), and 2) the general tendency for many types of emojis to appear in passage final position (Kwon et al., 2021). A defining characteristic of gestures is that they be precisely coordinated with the relevant message to be maximally effective at enhancing the focus on some elements relative to others (Overoye and Wilson, 2020). If emojis in text function like gestures in speech (Feldman et al., 2017; Gawne and McCulloch, 2019), then emojis of different functions may be easier to remember when they are positioned closer to relevant regions in the text.

6.2 Future Directions

Emoji position influences eye movement behaviors during reading (Feldman et al., 2019; Robus et al., 2020), however, it is unclear how emoji-text relation interacts with emoji position during reading. In the future, we plan to compare eye-tracking measures for the same emoji conditions used in the present study in different positions within passages. This will allow us to examine time-course and spill-over differences across conditions defined by the emoji-text relation. Additionally, future work should examine performance on a more challenging memory recognition task with a longer retention interval and more difficult emoji discrimination, as this approach may magnify the recognition memory effects found in the present study.

References

Eliza Barach, Laurie Beth Feldman, and Heather Sheridan. 2021. Are emojis processed like words?: Eye movements reveal the time course of semantic processing for emojified text. *Psychonomic Bulletin & Review*, 28(3):978–991.

Douglas Bates, Martin Mächler, Ben Bolker, and Steve Walker. 2015. Fitting linear mixed-effects models using lme4. *Journal of Statistical Software*, 67(1):1–48.

Elisabeth Beyersmann, Signy Wegener, and Nenagh Kemp. 2022. That's good news: Semantic congruency effects in emoji processing. *Journal of Media Psychology: Theories, Methods, and Applications*.

Christos Chatzichristos, Manuel Morante, Nikolaos Andreadis, Eleftherios Kofidis, Yiannis Kopsinis, and Sergios Theodoridis. 2020. Emojis influence autobiographical memory retrieval from reading words: An fmri-based study. *PloS one*, 15(7):e0234104.

Neil Cohn, Tim Roijackers, Robin Schaap, and Jan Engelen. 2018. Are emoji a poor substitute for words? sentence processing with emoji substitutions. In *Cognitive Science*, pages 1524–1529.

Fergus IM Craik and Robert S Lockhart. 1972. Levels of processing: A framework for memory research. *Journal of verbal learning and verbal behavior*, 11(6):671–684.

Fergus IM Craik and Endel Tulving. 1975. Depth of processing and the retention of words in episodic memory. *Journal of experimental Psychology: general*, 104(3):268–294.

Thomas A Daniel and Alecka L Camp. 2020. Emojis affect processing fluency on social media. *Psychology of Popular Media*, 9(2):208–213.

Laurie Beth Feldman, Cecilia R Aragon, Nan-Chen Chen, and Judith F Kroll. 2017. Emoticons in text may function like gestures in spoken or signed communication. *Behavioral and Brain Sciences*, 40.

Laurie Beth Feldman, Eliza Barach, and Heather Sheridan. 2019. Eye movement measures when reading pure and emojified text. *International workshop on Literacy and Writing systems: Cultural, Neuropsychological, and Psycholinguistic Perspectives*.

Scott H Fraundorf, Duane G Watson, and Aaron S Benjamin. 2010. Recognition memory reveals just how contrastive contrastive accenting really is. *Journal of memory and language*, 63(3):367–386.

Charlotte Garcia, Alexandra Ţurcan, Hannah Howman, and Ruth Filik. 2022. Emoji as a tool to aid the comprehension of written sarcasm: Evidence from younger and older adults. *Computers in Human Behavior*, 126:106971.

Lauren Gawne and Gretchen McCulloch. 2019. Emoji as digital gestures. *Language@ Internet*, 17(2).

Thomas Holtgraves and Caleb Robinson. 2020. Emoji can facilitate recognition of conveyed indirect meaning. *PloS one*, 15(4):e0232361.

Lauren A Homann, Brady RT Roberts, Sara Ahmed, and Myra A Fernandes. 2022. Are emojis processed visuo-spatially or verbally? evidence for dual codes. *Visual Cognition*, 30(4):267–279.

Walter Kintsch. 1988. The role of knowledge in discourse comprehension: a construction-integration model. *Psychological Review*, 95(2):163.

Jingun Kwon, Naoki Kobayashi, Hidetaka Kamigaito, Hiroya Takamura, and Manabu Okumura. 2021. Making your tweets more fancy: Emoji insertion to texts. In *Proceedings of the International Conference on Recent Advances in Natural Language Processing (RANLP 2021)*, pages 770–779.

Robert A Mason and Marcel Adam Just. 2004. How the brain processes causal inferences in text: A theoretical account of generation and integration component processes utilizing both cerebral hemispheres. *Psychological Science*, 15(1):1–7.

Acacia L Overoye and Margaret Wilson. 2020. Does gesture lighten the load? the case of verbal analogies. *Frontiers in psychology*, page 2388.

Pau A Packard, Antoni Rodríguez-Fornells, Nico Bunzeck, Berta Nicolás, Ruth de Diego-Balaguer, and Lluís Fuentemilla. 2017. Semantic congruence accelerates the onset of the neural signals of successful memory encoding. *Journal of Neuroscience*, 37(2):291–301.

Christopher M Robus, Christopher J Hand, Ruth Filik, and Melanie Pitchford. 2020. Investigating effects of emoji on neutral narrative text: Evidence from eye movements and perceived emotional valence. *Computers in human Behavior*, 109:106361.

Alison JS Sanford, Anthony J Sanford, Jo Molle, and Catherine Emmott. 2006. Shallow processing and attention capture in written and spoken discourse. *Discourse Processes*, 42(2):109–130.

Tatjana Scheffler, Lasse Brandt, Marie de la Fuente, and Ivan Nenchev. 2022. The processing of emoji-word substitutions: a self-paced-reading study. *Computers in Human Behavior*, 127:107076.

Sandra Virtue and Laura Motyka Joss. 2017. Hemispheric processing of predictive inferences: the influence of reading goals and textual constraint. *Cognitive Neuroscience*, 8(1):50–58.

Benjamin Weissman. 2019. Emojis in sentence processing: An electrophysiological approach. In *Companion Proceedings of The 2019 World Wide Web Conference*, pages 478–479.

Benjamin Weissman and Darren Tanner. 2018. A strong wink between verbal and emoji-based irony: How the brain processes ironic emojis during language comprehension. *PloS one*, 13(8):e0201727.

EmojiCloud: a Tool for Emoji Cloud Visualization

Yunhe Feng
University of Washington
yunhe@uw.edu

Cheng Guo
University of Washington
cguo3@uw.edu

Bingbing Wen
University of Washington
bingbw@uw.edu

Peng Sun
CUHK, Shenzhen
sunpengzju@gmail.com

Yufei Yue*
Amazon.com
heurekayue@gmail.com

Dingwen Tao
Washington State University
dingwen.tao@wsu.edu

Abstract

This paper proposes EmojiCloud, an open-source Python-based emoji cloud visualization tool, to generate a quick and straightforward understanding of emojis from the perspective of frequency and importance. EmojiCloud is flexible enough to support diverse drawing shapes, such as rectangles, ellipses, and image masked canvases. We also follow inclusive and personalized design principles to cover the unique emoji designs from seven emoji vendors (e.g., Twitter, Apple, and Windows) and allow users to customize plotted emojis and background colors. We hope EmojiCloud can benefit the whole emoji community due to its flexibility, inclusiveness, and customizability.

1 Introduction and Background

Emojis play a significant role in social business listening, sentiment analysis, cross-language communication, and politics. People from different language and cultural backgrounds love emojis and use them very frequently. According to a recent survey (Team, 2015), almost everyone online had experience in using emojis. It is important to generate a fast and straightforward understanding of emojis in many research and applications.

Inspired by the word cloud (Bielenberg and Zacher, 2005; Dubinko et al., 2007), which has be adopted as an effective way to visualize the frequency and importance of words in text mining, we thought the word cloud of emojis seemed to be a good solution. However, as shown in Figure 1, the word cloud will change and modify emojis' original and important features, such as colors ( ), directionalities ( ), and textures ( ). These inaccurate emoji representations may lead to misunderstanding. For example, when emojis are upside down, they turn into that conveys different sentiments and meanings. Also, miscolored emojis such as may cause the problem of personal identity representations.

In addition, the word cloud of emojis fails to capture the diversity of emoji appearances customized by emoji vendors. As different emoji renderings across viewing platforms may cause communication errors and diverse interpretations (Miller Hillberg et al., 2018; Miller et al., 2016), it is very important to support vendor-wise emoji visualization. Although several online platforms, such as Talkwalker[1], Slido[2], and Poll Everywhere[3], offer emoji cloud services for various needs, they are not open-source and fail to provide APIs or functions for flexible usages in text mining. Moreover, these services are just targeting one emoji cloud canvas shape and one emoji vendor respectively.

Figure 1: Word cloud of emojis

In this paper, we design and implement EmojiCloud, a counterpart of the word cloud for emoji visualization. Instead of plotting words, EmojiCloud draws emoji images in a clear and cloud-like fashion and keeps all detailed emojis features. EmojiCloud is flexible to support diverse canvases, such as rectangles, ellipses, and image-masked shapes. It also enables users to customize emoji clouds by specifying emoji vendors (e.g., Twitter, Google, and Apple) and individual self-made emoji images when creating emoji clouds. As the first open-source Python-based emoji cloud visualization tool (to our best knowledge), EmojiCloud facilitates the understanding of emojis and will bring broader impacts of emojis in many domains. We believe it is

*The work does not relate to his position at Amazon.

[1]https://www.talkwalker.com/blog/emoji-analysis-crack-consumer-code

[2]https://whatsnew.slido.com/en/say-it-with-an-emoji-

[3]https://blog.polleverywhere.com/emoji-quiz-online/

Proceedings of the The Fifth International Workshop on Emoji Understanding and Applications in Social Media, pages 69 - 74
July 14, 2022

a valuable and important tool to the emoji community and even the text mining community.

2 EmojiCloud Design & Implementation

This section presents emoji image preparation, EmojiCloud layout designs, and implementation.

2.1 Emoji Image Retrieval and Preprocessing

As emoji vendors, such as Twitter, Apple, and Google, can implement emoji designs into their products, emojis encoded with the same Unicode characters may demonstrate distinct appearances across platforms. To make EmojiCloud accurate and inclusive, we take emoji appearance variances across diverse vendors into consideration. Specifically, we propose an emoji image retrieval framework that collects cross-vendor emoji data from the official website of Unicode Full Emoji List[4]. The framework crawls and stores the latest emoji images provided by seven vendors (i.e., Apple, Google, Meta, Windows, Twitter, JoyPixels, and Samsung) automatically. Considering new emojis are always requested by users (Feng et al., 2019) and the Unicode Consortium releases new emojis every year accordingly, the proposed framework is able to check and download newly added emoji images when an emoji image cannot be found in local storage.

(a) Raw image (b) Bounding box (c) Unoccupied pos.

Figure 2: Preprocessing original emoji images by determining bounding boxes and marking unoccupied pixel positions (colored as black in Figure 2(c))

The retrieved emoji images need to be preprocessed to remove white-colored surrounding pixels that may cause a sparse emoji layout in EmojiCloud. As all retrieved emoji images are formatted in PNG, all these white-colored surrounding pixels have an alpha value of zero, representing full transparency. We propose a two-step transparency-based white space removal approach to reserve meaningful emoji pixels. First, as shown in Figure 2(b), we calculate the bounding box of an original emoji image by removing surrounding white-colored rows and columns. Second, within the bounding box, we mark the positions of pixels that are not part of the emoji representation (see the black pixels in Figure 2(c)) as unoccupied. We use E and U to represent the emoji image pixel values and the pixel unoccupied statuses, where $E_{x,y}$ represents the emoji pixel value at the coordinate (x, y) and $U_{x,y} \in \{0, 1\}$ indicates whether the pixel at (x, y) is unoccupied ($U_{x,y} = 1$) or not ($U_{x,y} = 0$). The above two image operations help create a compact emoji cloud layout. Note that white-colored pixels composing emoji representations, such as the white pixels inside the cooked rice emoji 🍚, are not touched because they have a positive alpha value.

[4]https://unicode.org/emoji/charts/full-emoji-list.html

2.2 EmojiCloud Layout Design

This section presents how to determine emoji sizes by frequency weights and design emoji layouts.

2.2.1 Emoji Size Calculation

We use a quintuple $e = (a, b, w, E, U)$ to represent an emoji, where a, b, w are the width, height, and edge-level frequency weight of emoji e. Recall that E and U represent pixel values and pixel unoccupied statuses. Suppose we have a list of emojis $\mathbf{e}$ to create an emoji cloud, where the ith emoji in $\mathbf{e}$ is expressed as $e_i = (a_i, b_i, w_i, E^i, U^i)$. The image sizes of all emojis have been standardized, i.e., $a_i * b_i = c; \forall i \in [1, |\mathbf{e}|]$, where c is a constant and $|\mathbf{e}|$ is the total count of emojis.

To ensure all emojis $\mathbf{e}$ can be drawn on the canvas without overlapping, we must adjust the weighted emoji plotting sizes with an edge rescale ratio r. Let's say the drawable emoji cloud canvas size is s. The rule of thumb is that r satisfies the following inequality.

$$s \geq \sum_{i=1}^{|\mathbf{e}|} w_i^2 * a_i * b_i * r^2 = \sum_{i=1}^{|\mathbf{e}|} w_i^2 * c * r^2 \quad (1)$$

where a *possible* maximum edge rescale ratio r can be $\sqrt{s/(c * \sum_{i=1}^{|\mathbf{e}|} w_i^2)}$. Thus, the rescaled width and height of emoji e_i are expressed as $a'_i = a_i * w_i * r$ and $b'_i = b_i * w_i * r$. The edge rescale ratio r decays at a rate of 0.9 if there is not enough room to plot all emojis on the canvas (see Line 36 in Algorithm 1).

2.2.2 Emoji Layout

Suppose we have a canvas with a $m * n$ rectangle bounding box in pixel. We use C and V to repre-

Algorithm 1: EmojiCloud Layout

1 **Input**: $\mathbf{e}$: a list of emojis; (m, n, s, C, V): a canvas with width m, height n, drawable size s, pixel values C, and pixel painting eligibility V on the canvas; c: the standardized size of emoji images;
2 **Output**: C: an emoji cloud image;
3 $\mathbf{e} \leftarrow$ sort the emoji list $\mathbf{e}$ by emoji weights $\mathbf{w} = [w_1, w_2, .., w_{|\mathbf{e}|}]$ in reverse order;
4 $r \leftarrow \sqrt{s/(c * \sum_{i=1}^{|\mathbf{e}|} w_i^2)}$; // rescale ratio in Equation 1
5 **for** $x = 1 \rightarrow m$ **do** // x coordinate of canvas
6   **for** $y = 1 \rightarrow n$ **do** // y coordinate of canvas
7   **if** $V_{x,y} = 1$ **then** // canvas pixel is eligible for painting
8   append (x, y) into the canvas pixel coordinate list $\mathbf{p_c}$; // build $\mathbf{p_c}$
9 $\mathbf{p_c} \leftarrow$ sort $\mathbf{p_c}$ by the Euclidean distance between $(x, y) \in \mathbf{p_c}$ and the canvas center $(m/2, n/2)$;
10 $count \leftarrow 0$; // count of plotted emojis
11 **while** $count < |\mathbf{e}|$ **do** // not all emoji have been plotted
12   $count \leftarrow 0$; // no emoji has been plotted
13   **for** $i = 1 \rightarrow |\mathbf{e}|$ **do** // iterate the emojis sorted by weights in reverse order
14     $(a_i, b_i, w_i, E^i, U^i) \leftarrow e_i$; // parse e_i into its quintuple representation
15     $a'_i \leftarrow a_i * w_i * r$; $b'_i \leftarrow b_i * w_i * r$; // rescale width and height of e_i
16     $E^{i'}, U^{i'} \leftarrow$ update E^i, U^i based on r ; // rescale E^i, U^i based on r
17   **for** $(x, y) \in \mathbf{p_c}$ **do** // (x, y) is where the center of e_i to be located
18       $flag \leftarrow True$; // indicate the possibility of plotting e_i
19       $\mathbf{p_t} \leftarrow [\ ]$; // a list of canvas temporal coordinates to plot e_i
20   **for** $x' = 1 \rightarrow a$ **do** // x coordinate of emoji image
21   **for** $y' = 1 \rightarrow b$ **do** // y coordinate of emoji image
22   **if** $U^{i'}_{x',y'} = 0$ **then** // emoji pixel (x', y') is not unoccupied
23             $x_o \leftarrow x' - a'_i/2$; $y_o \leftarrow y' - b'_i/2$; // the offsets to e_i center
24             $x_t \leftarrow x + x_o$; $y_t \leftarrow y + y_o$; // canvas temporal coordinate for e_i
25   append (x_t, y_t) to $\mathbf{p_t}$;
26   **if** $V_{x_t,y_t} = 0$ **then** // canvas pixel is not eligible for painting
27               $flag \leftarrow False$; // no room to plot e_i at (x, y)
28   break; // iterate the next $(x, y) \in \mathbf{p_c}$
29   **if** *flag* = *True* **then** // the emoji e_i can be plot at (x, y)
30   **for** $(x_t, y_t) \in \mathbf{p_t}$ **do** // iterate temporal pixel coordinates
31           $C_{x_t,x_t} \leftarrow E^{i'}_{x_t - x + a'_i/2, y_t - y + b'_i/2}$; // plot emoji e_i
32           $V_{x_t,y_t} \rightarrow 0$; // set painting eligibility as negative
33   remove (x_t, y_t) from $\mathbf{p_c}$; // delete (x_t, y_t) for computing efficiency
34         $count \leftarrow count + 1$; // increase the number of plotted emoji by 1
35   break;
36   $r \leftarrow r * 0.9$; // decay the edge rescale ratio by 0.9
37 **return** C

sent pixel values and the pixel painting eligibility on the canvas. To be more specific, $C_{x,y}$ represents canvas pixel values at the coordinate (x, y) and $V_{x,y} \in \{0, 1\}$ indicates the painting eligibility of (x, y), where $x \in [1, m]$ and $y \in [1, n]$. The design of V controls the drawable shape (e.g., a circle or an ellipse) on the canvas (see section 2.3 for details). As it is possible that not all pixel coordinates are eligible for painting, the drawable canvas size s in Equation 1 does not always equal to $m * n$. Thus, a canvas can be expressed as (m, n, s, C, V).

For aesthetic purposes, we arrange an emoji with a larger weight (indicting more importance) closer to the canvas center, where more attention is usually given. First, we sort the emoji list e based on their corresponding weights in reverse order (see Line 3 in Algorithm 1). Then, we sort $\mathbf{p_c}$, a list of canvas pixel coordinates (x, y) that are eligible for painting emojis (i.e., $V_{x,y} = 1$), by their Euclidean distances to the canvas center $(m/2, n/2)$. For each sorted emoji $e_i \in \mathbf{e}$, we rescale its original representation $(a_i, b_i, w_i, E^i, U^i)$ into $(a'_i, b'_i, w'_i, E^{i'}, U^{i'})$ using the edge rescale ratio r.

Next, we attempt to draw emoji e starting from the canvas pixel coordinate $(x, y) \in \mathbf{p_c}$ that is closest to the center of the canvas. As the center $(a'_i/2, b'_i/2)$ of emoji e will be mapped at (x, y) on the canvas, the rest emoji pixel coordinate (x', y') will be mapped at $(x_t = x + x_o, y_t = y + y_o)$, where

x_o and y_o are offsets of $x' - a_i'/2$ and $y' - b_i'/2$. If any occupied emoji pixel coordinate (x', y') (i.e., $U^{i'}_{x',y'} = 0$) fails to be mapped to the canvas coordinate (x_t, y_t) (i.e., $V_{x_t,y_t} = 0$), we continue to check the next canvas pixel coordinate that is the second most closest to the center of canvas (see Line 17-28 in Algorithm 1).

When emoji e_i can be plotted successfully on the canvas ($flag = True$), we copy and paste each pixel value in $E^{i'}$ into the canvas C. In addition, the painting eligibilities of the involved pixel coordinates on the canvas are set as 0. For computing efficiency, we delete corresponding pixel coordinates from the sorted $\mathbf{p_c}$ and increase the count of plotted emojis (see Line 29-35 in Algorithm 1).

2.3 Canvas Design

The proposed EmojiCloud is flexible to support diverse drawable canvas shapes, including rectangle, ellipse, image-masked, and arbitrary canvases.

2.3.1 Default Canvas

We set the default canvas shape as an $m * n$ rectangle, and all pixel coordinates within the rectangle are eligible to draw emojis. The painting eligibility $V_{x,y}$ is set as 1 for all $x \in [1, m]$ and $y \in [1, n]$.

2.3.2 Ellipse Canvas

Suppose we have a drawable ellipse area within an $m * n$ rectangle bounding box for plotting emojis. The semi-major and semi-minor axes' lengths are expressed as $m/2$ and $n/2$. The center pixel coordinate is expressed as $(m/2, n/2)$. If pixel coordinate (x, y) on canvas satisfies the following inequality, $V_{x,y}$ is set as 1.

$$(\frac{x - \frac{m}{2}}{\frac{m}{2}})^2 + (\frac{y - \frac{n}{2}}{\frac{n}{2}})^2 \leq 1 \quad (2)$$

Otherwise, the coordinate (x, y) is outside of the ellipse, and the corresponding $V_{x,y}$ is set as 0. When m equals n, a circle canvas is defined.

2.3.3 Masked Canvas

EmojiCloud also allows users to specify a masked canvas based on a PNG background image. Similar to the emoji image preprocessing in Section 2.1, we first determine a $m * n$ bounding box of the image by removing the surrounding transparent pixels. Then we detect the image contour and draw a boundary accordingly (e.g., converting into). To be more specific, we scan the alpha values of pixels in the preprocessed image by row and by column respectively. Recall that the alpha channel in PNG controls pixel transparency. During the scanning, we identify pixels that cause a alpha value change greater than a threshold θ (by default $\theta = 10$) as boundary pixels. After all boundary pixels are determined, they will be colored by specified colors. If one pixel coordinate (x, y) is inside the boundary, the corresponding $V_{x,y}$ is set as 1.

2.3.4 Arbitrary Canvas

Users are allowed to specify arbitrary canvas drawable shapes by configuring the painting eligibility $V_{x,y}$ for pixel coordinate (x, y) on the canvas.

2.4 EmojiCloud Inclusive Design

EmojiCloud is flexible and inclusive to handle emoji images designed by seven vendors (i.e., Apple, Google, Meta, Windows, Twitter, JoyPixels, and Samsung.) We provide an option for users to specify the vendor of interest. In addition, users can customize and combine emojis based on their requirements. For example, a red apple emoji (U+1F34E) can be replaced by for marketing campaigns. The sauropod (U+1F995) and T-Rex emoji (U+1F996) can be combined as if it is not necessary to distinguish dinosaur species.

2.5 Implementation and Open Source

We develop open-source EmojiCloud in Python, one of the most popular programming languages for natural language processing and text mining. EmojiCloud has been packaged as a Python library and published through Python Package Index (PyPI). Users can run *pip install **EmojiCloud*** to install the EmojiCloud package and use *from **EmojiCloud** import **EmojiCloud*** to call for EmojiCloud functions in Python scripts. An EmojiCloud tutorial is available at `https://pypi.org/project/EmojiCloud/`.

3 EmojiCloud Evaluation

In this section, we demonstrate that EmojiCloud is able to support diverse canvas shapes, different emoji vendors, and customized emoji images.

3.1 Visualization on Different Canvases

EmojiCloud allows users to select the drawable canvas shapes to generate emoji cloud images. As shown in Figure 3, we plot an identical list of emojis (with the same weights) on rectangle, ellipse, and image masked canvases. Emojis with large weights are placed as close to the canvas center as possible. To make the emoji cloud image compact, emojis with small weights can also be placed near the canvas center if there is enough room.

(a) Rectangle (b) Ellipse (c) Mask

Figure 3: EmojiCloud on different canvases

3.2 Visualization for Different Emoji Vendors

EmojiCloud is flexible to cover seven different emoji vendors. Users can specify the vendor when creating EmojiCloud images. Figure 4 shows the generated EmojiCloud images of the same emoji list for Twitter, Apple, Google, Windows, JoyPixels, Meta, and Samsung. Although vendors demonstrate different layout patterns, heavy-weight emojis are always placed in the center zone, where people usually pay more attention.

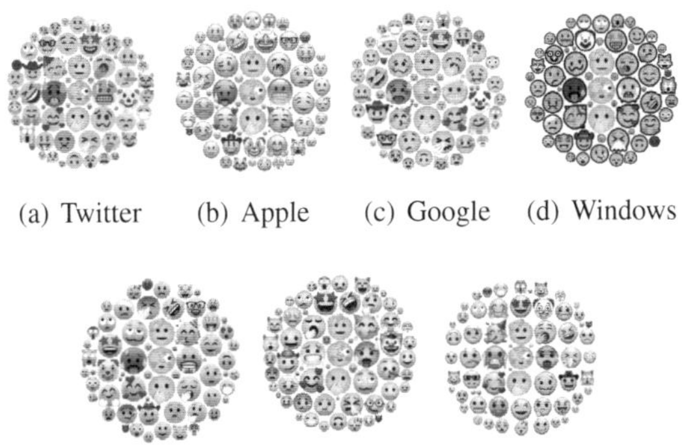

(a) Twitter (b) Apple (c) Google (d) Windows

(e) JoyPixels (f) Meta (g) Samsung

Figure 4: EmojiCloud for different vendors

3.3 Visualization of Customized Emojis

Besides the above seven vendors, EmojiCloud supports arbitrary emoji representations designed and specified by users. Figure 5 demonstrates an EmojiCloud case of FIFA World Cup, where the default trophy (U+1F3C6) 🏆 is customized by . Also, EmojiCloud allows users to customize the canvas background (see the color of grass on soccer fields in Figure 5). Customized emojis make EmojiCloud more appropriate and accurate to depict the investigated case studies.

3.4 Running Time Evaluation

The running time of EmojiCloud depends on how many emojis are plotted and the emoji cloud canvas

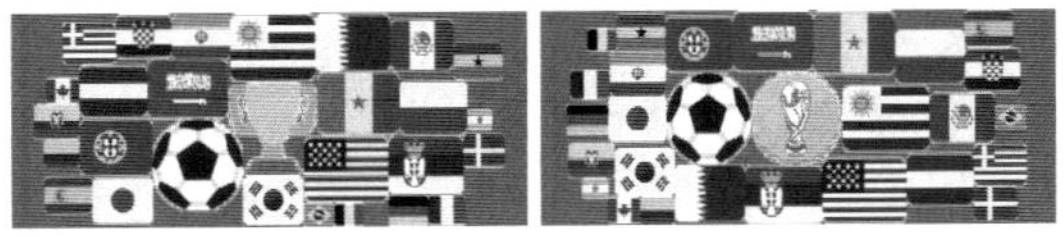

(a) Original (b) Customized

Figure 5: EmojiCloud for FIFA World Cup Trophy

size. We measured the running time of EmojiCloud on a laptop with an AMD Ryzen 7 4800HS processor and 16 GB RAM. We evaluated the emoji count from 25 to 60 with an increasing step of 5 on canvases of 300*300, 400*400, and 500*500 pixels. EmojiCloud with the same setting ran 10 times to ensure the running time was accurate. As shown in Figure 6, the running time generally increases as emoji counts and canvas sizes increase. An emoji cloud (containing up to 60 emojis) on a 300*300 pixels canvas can be generated within 5 seconds.

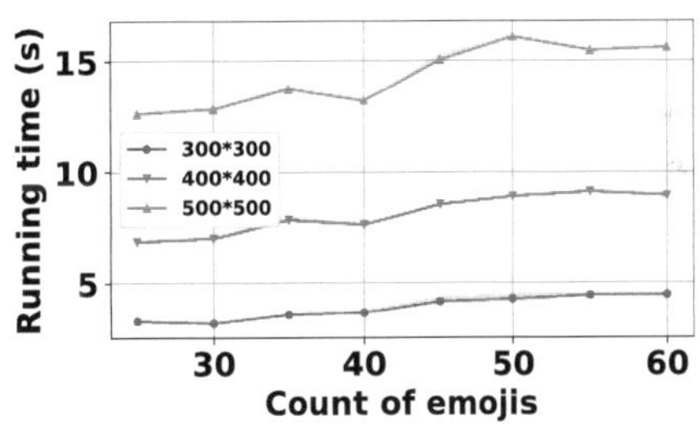

Figure 6: Running time of EmojiCloud

4 Conclusion and Future Work

We propose and develop open-source EmojiCloud to visualize a cluster of emojis according to associated frequency weights. EmojiCloud enables a novel and informative way to investigate emojis in natural language processing and text mining. We think EmojiCloud will benefit the whole emoji community due to its flexibility, inclusiveness, and customizability.

In the future, we will keep updating the open-source EmojiCloud based on the users' feedback, such as adding new functions and covering more emoji vendors. To further improve the flexibility and convenience of EmojiCloud, we will provide an online EmojiCloud service via `www.emojicloud.org`. In addition, we will explore the possibility of merging words and emojis in a unified word-emoji cloud.

References

Kai Bielenberg and Marc Zacher. 2005. Groups in social software: Utilizing tagging to integrate individual contexts for social navigation. *Digital Media. Bremen, Germeny, University Bremen. Master of Science in Digital Media*, 120.

Micah Dubinko, Ravi Kumar, Joseph Magnani, Jasmine Novak, Prabhakar Raghavan, and Andrew Tomkins. 2007. Visualizing tags over time. *ACM Transactions on the Web (TWEB)*, 1(2):7–es.

Yunhe Feng, Wenjun Zhou, Zheng Lu, Zhibo Wang, and Qing Cao. 2019. The world wants mangoes and kangaroos: A study of new emoji requests based on thirty million tweets. In *The World Wide Web Conference*, pages 2722–2728.

Hannah Jean Miller, Jacob Thebault-Spieker, Shuo Chang, Isaac Johnson, Loren Terveen, and Brent Hecht. 2016. "blissfully happy" or "ready tofight": Varying interpretations of emoji. In *Tenth international AAAI conference on web and social media*.

Hannah Miller Hillberg, Zachary Levonian, Daniel Kluver, Loren Terveen, and Brent Hecht. 2018. What i see is what you don't get: The effects of (not) seeing emoji rendering differences across platforms. *Proceedings of the ACM on Human-Computer Interaction*, 2(CSCW):1–24.

Emogi Research Team. 2015. *Emoji Report*.

Graphicon Evolution on the Chinese Social Media Platform BiliBili

Yiqiong Zhang
Guangdong University of Foreign Studies, China
zhangyiqiong@gdufs.edu.cn

Susan C. Herring
Indiana University Bloomington USA
herring@indiana.edu

Suifu Gan
Jinan University China
657742829@qq.com

Abstract

This study examines the evolutionary trajectory of graphicons in a 13-year corpus of comments from BiliBili, a popular Chinese video-sharing platform. Findings show that emoticons (kaomoji) rose and fell in frequency, while emojis and stickers are both presently on the rise. Graphicon distributions differ in comments and replies to comments. There is also a strong correlation between the types of graphicons used in comments and their corresponding replies, suggesting a priming effect. Finally, qualitative analysis of the 10 most-frequent kaomojis, emojis, and stickers reveals a trend for each successive graphicon type to become less about emotion expression and more integrated with platform-specific culture and the Chinese language. These findings lend partial support to claims in the literature about graphicon evolution.

1 Introduction

Graphicons are graphical icons used in text-based computer-mediated communication (Herring & Dainas, 2017). From the first use of :-) in 1982 (Evans, 2017) to the varied and colorful stickers on social media today, graphicons have changed dramatically. ASCII emoticons, the first graphicons, were composed of keyboard symbols and were typically used for expressing emotion. Emoticons in the Western context emphasize the mouth and are read at a 90-degree angle to the words (e.g., :-) for a smiley), while kaomoji (literally 'face letters'), a style of emoticon that arose in Japan and also became popular in China, are read in-line with words and emphasize the eyes (e.g., ^_^ or ^^) (Katsuno & Yano, 2002). Kaomojis express not only emotions, but also actions, objects, and story lines.[1]

Emojis were adopted globally after Apple included them in the iPhone in 2010 (Danesi, 2016). Emoji are more colorful, more representational (as opposed to schematic), and express a wider array of concepts than ASCII emoticons. Stickers, which were introduced a few years after emojis, take these trends further (Konrad et al., 2020). Usually larger than emoticons and emojis, stickers may include text; this is typical of stickers used on Chinese social media (e.g., see the examples in de Seta, 2018; Ge, 2020). Stickers are character-driven illustrations or animations that are typically offered as thematic sets on social media platforms (de Seta, 2018), although social media users in China may also create their own stickers (Ge, 2020).

Extensive studies have addressed the meaning, function, and usage of each type of graphicon in different cultural contexts (e.g., Al Rashdi, 2018; Ge, 2020; Ge & Herring, 2018; Logi & Zappavigna, 2021; Sampietro, 2019). Interrelations among the three types, however, have not attracted much attention until recently. Studies have explored the uses of the three graphicon types (de Seta, 2018), user perceptions of the three types (Tang & Hew, 2018), and the evolutionary trends they follow (Konrad et al., 2020). While these studies provide rich insights, the first two mainly used qualitative methods, and the latter analyzed contemporary data, despite making diachronic claims. Their findings remain to be verified by empirical comparison of graphicon use in longitudinal data.

2 Background

2.1 Graphicon evolution

As graphicons continue to grow in popularity worldwide and shape social media and mobile communications, it is important to understand

[1] http://kaomoji.ru/en/, retrieved April 5, 2022.

Proceedings of the The Fifth International Workshop on Emoji Understanding and Applications in Social Media, pages 75 - 85
July 14, 2022

how and why they evolve, and the implications of their evolution for where they are headed in the future. Konrad et al. (2020) posit that graphicons tend to follow an evolutionary trajectory consisting of three phases: an early phase, a high (or peak) phase, and a phase of decline and/or conventionalization. One of the main criteria for determining which phase a graphicon is currently in is frequency of use; another is pragmatic changes in graphicon use. For Western graphicons, according to Konrad et al. (2020), emoticons are in the third phase, emoji are in the second phase, and stickers are in the first phase. The authors predict that emoji will eventually reach the third phase, following the path of emoticons, and that stickers may eventually reach the second (and eventually the third) phase and overtake emoji in popularity.

The history of ASCII emoticons and emoji provide evidence in partial support of this trajectory. Pavalanathan and Eisenstein (2016) analyzed emoticons and emoji on Twitter in the 17 months after emoji were first introduced on the platform. They found that emoticon use dramatically decreased as emoji use increased. Furthermore, a number of studies have reported that emoticons have become conventionalized as a type of punctuation (Markman & Oshima, 2007; Provine et al., 2007). That is, emoticons have declined in frequency of use and have become conventionalized, evidence that they are in the third phase of Konrad et al.'s (2020) evolutionary trajectory. Meanwhile, emojis in the West remain at the peak of their popularity.

While this evidence is compelling, it is limited. As yet no comparable evidence exists for all three graphicon types, or for the relationship of emojis to stickers. Konrad et al. (2020) interviewed and surveyed Facebook Messenger users about their use of emoji and stickers, identifying many areas of overlap in function of the two graphicons. They also noted some differences: participants described emojis as better suited for expressing emotion, whereas stickers were considered more specific and better at expressing the user's personality. However, Konrad et al. (2020) did not quantify emoji and sticker use over time. What is needed is a longitudinal corpus of data involving the use of emoticons, emojis, and stickers, in order to be able to map the evolutionary trajectory of the three types of graphicons.

2.2 Graphicon on Chinese social media

Graphicons on Chinese social media are distinctive in their design and usage. They are designed in creative ways by and for Chinese social media users to enliven conversations (Ge, 2020), resolve the tension between the openness of social media and constraint-bounded social norms (Zhang et al., 2021), and playfully subvert reality and avoid internet surveillance and censorship (Li & Zhu, 2019). The design of graphicons carries rich cultural messages (de Seta, 2018) and interacts with the Chinese national character (Li & Zhu, 2019).

Users of Chinese social media use the umbrella term 表情 *Biaoqing* (a contraction of 表达情感 'expressing emotions') for all types of graphicons, suggesting a popular understanding of the shared usage of graphicons for emotion expression (de Seta, 2018). Yet different types of *Biaoqing* are distinguished. Kaomojis were introduced to Chinese users in the mid-1990s; emojis were first used in the early 2000s in Chinese discussion boards, instant messaging services, and social networking web sites; and stickers first became available on the QQ and WeChat platforms in 2012 (de Seta, 2018). As in the West, all three types of graphicons are currently available for use.

In terms of frequency of use, Konrad et al. (2020) suggest that graphicon evolution is more advanced in Asia than in the West. They predict that stickers should be catching up with or surpassing emoji use in Asia, in contrast to the West, where stickers are still much less popular than emojis. The evidence to support this prediction so far is limited and primarily anecdotal. Fifteen years ago, Markman and Oshima (2007) reported that the use of kaomojis as punctuation was more conspicuous in Japan than the United States. Emojis are used more frequently by Chinese social media users compared to their Western counterparts (Zhang et al., 2014); however, comparable statistics about the frequency of sticker use have not been found. Several studies have pointed out that stickers are now very popular among Chinese social media users (e.g., de Seta, 2018; Ge, 2020), but their frequency has not been compared with that of emojis. In this paper, we quantify the relative frequency of the three different types of graphicons in Chinese social media over time.

2.3 Research questions

Based on the gaps delineated in the above literature review, this study addresses the following research questions:

RQ1: What are the relative frequencies of each type of Chinese graphicon, and how have their frequencies changed over time?

RQ2: What trends are evident from the most frequently-used graphicons of each type?

3 Methodology

3.1 Data

Our corpus is composed of 13 years of longitudinal data from the BiliBili platform. BiliBili is a video-sharing platform that, like YouTube, allows users to post comments below the videos and also features short *danmu* messages that are overlaid on the video itself.

The BiliBili platform was chosen for several reasons. First, it is one of the most popular Chinese social media platforms. The users of the platform are mainly under the age of 35,[2] and its average monthly active users reached 272 million (almost one-fifth of the Chinese population) by the end of 2021.[3] Second, the comments can include emoticons, emojis, and stickers (although stickers did not become available on the platform until 2016). Third, BiliBili is well-established, having been launched in 2009 as a platform for sharing ACG-related (Anime, Comics, and Games) content,[4] and it has expanded over the years to cover more general topics. Last and most relevant for this study, the platform preserves a historical record of the comments posted below the videos, including the graphicons in the comments, and the comments can be captured automatically. We considered other popular Chinese social media platforms (e.g., Sina Weibo, WeChat) as possible data sources, but none of them would have allowed automatic capturing of longitudinal data containing all three graphicon types.

The data consist of comments and replies to comments (hereafter, replies) from the channel of BiliBili's annual Spring Festival Gala Show (hereafter, the BiliBili show).[5] This channel was chosen because it is the only one that includes comments dating back to 2010, and the comments are all on videos on the same topic. The BiliBili show started in 2010 and soon became an important annual event on the platform.[6] The show consists of a mash-up video of content provided by professional users to celebrate the Chinese New Year, and is released on the eve of the Chinese New Year. It is considered by BiliBili users to be the online equivalent of the Spring Festival Gala produced by the China Media Group, which is broadcast annually on Chinese New Year's Eve and has the largest audience of any entertainment show in the world. Besides the show videos, the BiliBili show channel includes a number of videos related to the gala show, such as trailers, teasers, and outtakes. These videos include older comments and replies, like the gala show videos do, and are thus included in our data.

Comments and replies from all 42 videos available in the channel, covering the years from 2010 to 2022, were captured and stored in February 2022 using Python and the Scrapy tool. A total of 1,031,183 messages (including both comments and replies) were collected.

3.2 Methods

The three types of graphicons in the corpus were identified using different methods. The emoticons in our corpus are Japanese-style kaomoji. The recognition of kaomojis was carried out by a semi-supervised process of deep learning and manual identification. Manual annotation of kaomojis in a sample corpus was done, and this was used to train deep learning models of BiLSTM and CRF (Qin et al., 2019) to learn and develop a list of kaomoji types. Kaomoji types identified by the algorithm were checked manually. Three rounds of manual and machine iteration were conducted before a final set of kaomoji types was obtained for the purpose of examining kaomoji use in the corpus.

The set of sticker types was developed based on the package of BiliBili stickers available on GitHub.[7] The set of Yellow Faces [小黄脸] from the GitHub sticker package (see Figure 1)

[2] https://socialbeta.com/t/reports-bilibili-marketing-planning-2021-02-22, retrieved April 4, 2022.

[3] https://m.jiemian.com/article/7167482.html, retrieved April 4, 2022.

[4] https://zh.wikipedia.org/wiki/Bilibili, retrieved April 4, 2022.

[5] https://space.bilibili.com/1868902080

[6] https://www.bilibili.com/read/cv1069082, retrieved April 5, 2022.

[7] https://github.com/amtoaer/bilibili-stickers, retrieved February 25, 2022. The GitHub collection was updated on January 31, 2022; all comments and replies in our data were

Figure 1: Examples from the set of Yellow Faces.

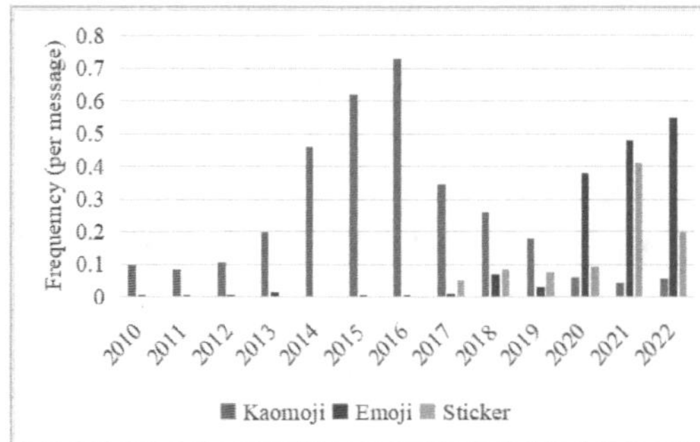

Figure 2: Frequencies (tokens) of three graphicons.

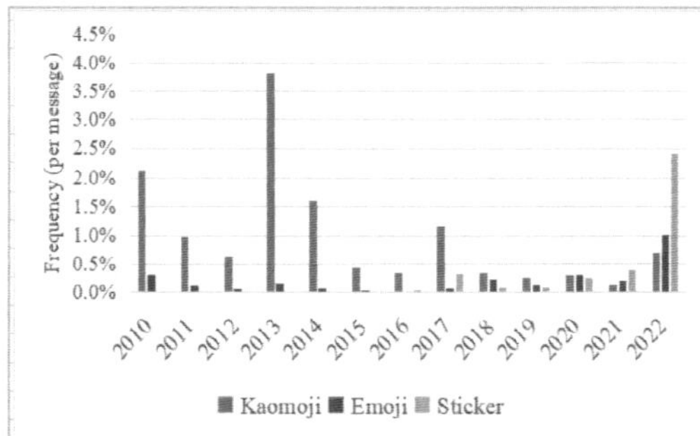

Figure 3: Frequencies (types) of three graphicons.

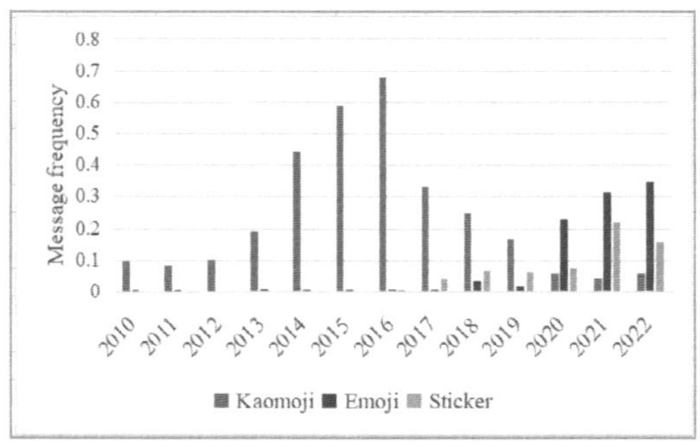

Figure 4: Frequencies of messages containing at least one graphicon.

contains a number of graphicons that we reclassified as emojis, as described below. The set includes three kinds of images: 1) iconic representations of objects (e.g., Koi [锦鲤], the second from the top left in Figure 1); 2) yellow faces that are more elaborated than Unicode emojis (e.g., Astonished face [惊讶], the second from the top right; and 3) stickers that are character-driven (e.g., the Laigu [来古] series of three girls expressing contemplation [沉思] (the third from the bottom right), dullness [呆滞] (second from the bottom right), and doubt [疑问] (bottom right). However, the iconic images and yellow faces are displayed in the corpus the same size as emojis, which are smaller than stickers, and they are not character-driven. Therefore, we removed them from the sticker package and added them to the set of emojis prior to analysis. The set of emojis also includes Unicode emojis from the Python emoji module with a character length of 1.

Using the above methods, a list of the three types of graphicons was derived for obtaining graphicon occurrences in the corpus. The frequencies of graphicon types and tokens in each year were obtained. We also conducted a thematic content analysis of the 10 most frequently occurring graphicons of each type in the corpus.

4 Findings

The findings are presented in two parts. The first part reports the frequency distribution of the graphicons over time. The second part presents a qualitative analysis of the most frequently used graphicons in terms of what they suggest about trends in Chinese graphicon evolution.

4.1 Frequency distribution of graphicons

Three types of graphicon were identified in the corpus: kaomoji, emoji and sticker. Definitions and descriptions of each types are provided in the Introduction and in Section 3.2.

The frequency of each graphicon type was normalized as a ratio in relation to the number of messages in the corpus. This was done because some messages lack text and include only graphicons. Normalized frequencies of all graphicon tokens for each of the 13 years are shown in Figure 2, and normalized frequencies of graphicon types are in Figure 3.

These statistics provide partial support for the evolutionary trajectory proposed by Konrad et al. (2020). The use of kaomojis shows a clear trajectory of an early phase, a high phase, and decline. The peak of kaomoji tokens appears in

made after that. We manually confirmed that the Github package included all the stickers in our corpus.

2016, and the peak of kaomoji types comes earlier in 2013.

Moreover, kaomojis have been replaced by emojis and stickers. Emojis experienced a dramatic increase in occurrences in the most recent three years (the red bars in 2020, 2021 and 2022 in Figure 2), and the types of emoji also show a notable uptick in 2022 (the red bars in 2020, 2021 and 2022 in Figure 3). The picture for stickers is somewhat less clear. After stickers appeared on BiliBili in 2016, their usage increased and rose sharply in 2021. Although the frequency of sticker tokens dropped off in 2022, the types increased steeply. That is, fewer stickers were used in 2022 than in 2021, yet many more varieties of stickers appear in the 2022 data.

It is possible that stickers use has started to decline in 2022. But it is also possible that the sharp rise in 2021 is due to unconventional usage of graphicons by the large number of new users who joined BiliBili during the Covid-19 pandemic. User numbers increased by 55% to 202 million in 2020,[8] as a result of intensive branding promotion of the platform.[9] The new users might have initially used stickers more frequently than older users but gradually accommodated their graphicon use to the norms of the community.

The frequencies of messages (comments or replies) that contain at least one of the three types of graphicon is shown in Figure 4. The nearly identical pattern of kaomojis in Figure 2 and Figure 4 suggests that a kaomoji was mostly used only once per message. However, two or more emojis are commonly used in a message. In the statistics from 2022, for example, 55 emojis appear per 100 messages (the red bar in 2022 in Figure 2), but these emoji only appear in 35% of the messages (the red bar in 2022 in Figure 4). Stickers tend to be used once per message in early years (see the similar frequencies in 2016-2020), but they are used on average more than once in 2021 (41 stickers appear per 100 messages, but they appear in only 22% of the messages).

Further, graphicon usage differs in comments and replies, as summarized in Figure 5. Kaomojis and stickers appear more frequently in comments, while emojis are used with similar frequency in comments and replies.

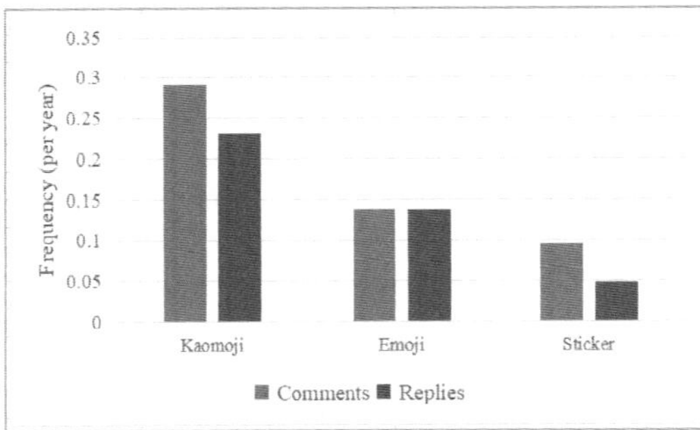

Figure 5: Frequencies (tokens) of three graphicons in comments and replies.

Note: The calculation excludes the data from the years 2010 and 2011, since there were no replies in those years.

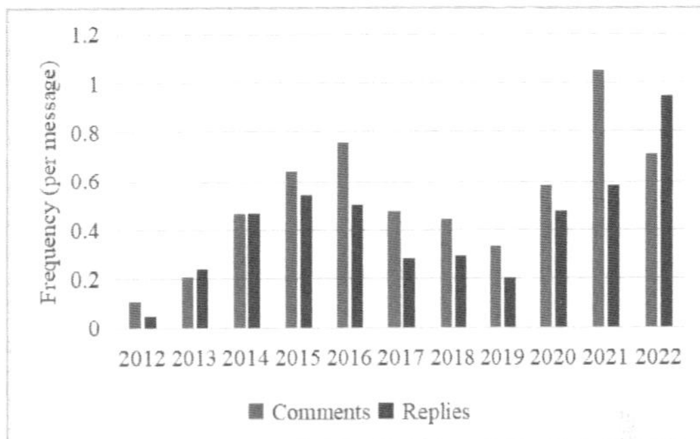

Figure 6: Frequencies of graphicon use in comments and replies.

Note: No replies were made in 2010 and 2011.

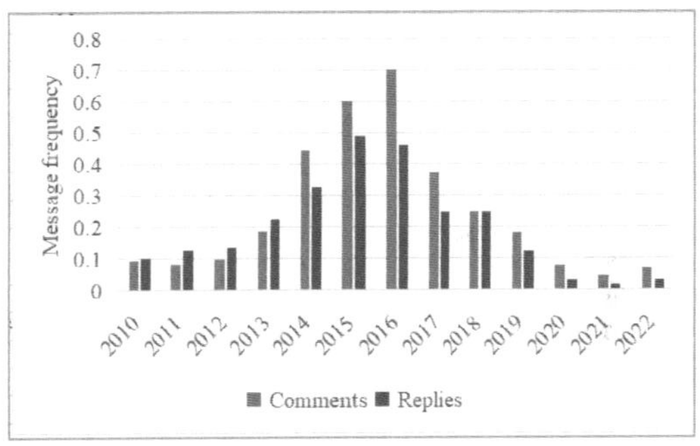

Figure 7: Frequencies of comments and replies containing at least one kaomoji.

Meanwhile, as displayed in Figure 6, a consistent pattern is found whereby more graphicons were used in comments than in replies every year except for 2022. It is also worth noting that stickers were available on the platform in 2016, but they were not used in replies until 2018; the reasons for this lag are unclear.

[8] Graphicon usage of commenters who joined in 2020 is reflected in the data of 2021. This is because the show was released in January 2021, and a majority of comments was made within the first month of the video release.

[9] https://www.sohu.com/a/452506920_153054, retrieved April 7, 2022.

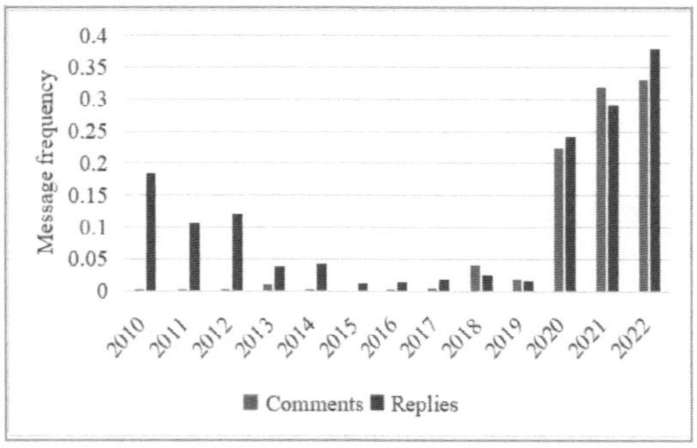

Figure 8: Frequencies of comments and replies containing at least one emoji.

Another interesting phenomenon is the strong correlation between the frequency of each graphicon type in the comments and their corresponding replies. This is evident for kaomojis in Figure 7 and for emojis in Figure 8. Frequencies for stickers are not presented here because stickers were not available on BiliBili until 2016. The years of the replies in Figures 7 & 8 refer to the year when the corresponding comments were made rather than the year when the replies were made (as in Figure 6). For instance, for a reply made in 2022 to a comment from 2010, the year of the reply was counted as 2010 in Figures 7 & 8 but counted as 2022 in Figure 6. The frequencies of kaomoji usage in comments and replies (Figure 7) show a very similar pattern; the correlation is 0.93. The frequencies of emojis (Figure 8) show a less consistent pattern, but the correlation between comments and replies is still strong at 0.89. The strong correlations between graphicon usage in comments and replies suggest a "priming effect" (Molden, 2014) of graphicon usage, meaning that the occurrences of graphicons in comments have an impact on the usage of graphicons in corresponding replies.

4.2 The top 10 graphicons

Next, we qualitatively examined the most frequently occurring graphicons in the corpus. The top 10 occurrences of each graphicon in each category are listed in Table 1. In general, the progression from kaomojis to emojis to stickers reveals a trend of movement from general emotion expression to meanings localized in the discourse practices of the BiliBili platform.

Kaomojis are borrowed from Japanese to express emotions, and indeed, the most frequently used kaomoji types in our corpus mainly express emotion. Four kaomojis express joy (Nos. 3, 4, 7 & 10). Five kaomojis perform actions with incorporated affect (Nos. 1, 5, 6, 8 & 9). There is no explicit encoding of affect in the kaomojis of cheering (No. 1) or dancing with music (No. 6), but these two actions are strongly conventionally associated with a happy mood.

In contrast, fewer of the 10 most popular emojis focus on emotions. Rather, several of the emojis reference culture-specific information about the New Year's celebration event and the BiliBili platform. Four emojis (Nos. 2, 6, 7 & 9) are for the Chinese new year celebration. Two of them (Nos. 6 & 9) integrate the shape of a TV set, the icon that symbolizes BiliBili, in their design (see Nos. 4 & 5 in stickers). It is worth noting that only one of the popular emojis are Unicode emojis (No. 7, Sparkles), supporting previous findings that platform-specific sets of graphicons are more popular in China than Unicode emojis (de Seta, 2018; Y. Zhang et al., 2021). Even the Unicode (Sparkles) emoji is localized in meaning, in that it is frequently used in Chinese New Year's wishes as a symbolic representation of firecrackers.

Integration with platform discourse practices is most evident in stickers. Four stickers belong to the Popular Words Series (Nos. 1, 2, 3 & 8), which are graphic representations of selected popular expressions from comments or *danmu* (messages that are overlaid on the video itself). In addition, the stickers include two variants of the platform's icon (Nos. 4 & 5 in the "Tiny TV" set) and two virtual spokespersons of BiliBili[10] (Nos. 6 & 10 in the "2233 Girls" set).

The themes expressed by the three types of graphicons are summarized in Table 2. Emotion expression becomes less prominent as we move from kaomoji to emoji and to sticker. In contrast, references to platform discourse and the integration of Chinese characters become more apparent as we move from the older to the newer graphicons. Relatedly, action decreases somewhat. For most of the themes, emoji serves as a transition between kaomoji and sticker.

[10] https://www.bilibili.com/read/cv1069082, retrieved April 5, 2022.

	Kaomojis	Meaning	Freq	Emojis	Meaning	Freq	Stickers	Meaning	Freq
1	-(°- °)つロ	Cheers	108691		Playful dog face	28495	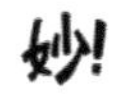	PWS: Wonderful	27179
2	(=・ω・=)	Cat	19217		Being blessed	19420		PWS: Hooray	16853
3	(￣▽￣)	Joy	14668		Cheering for someone	6603		PWS: Obtaining trivia	8041
4	(｀・ω・´)	Joy	12815		Wonderful	6077		Tiny TV set: smile	4920
5	(°∀°)ﾉ	Greeting happily	11427		Smile	5740		Tiny TV set: like	4439
6	(~￣△￣)~	Dancing with music	7319		Year of the Ox	5599		2233 girls: laugh out loud	4369
7	(⌒▽⌒)	Joy	6642		Sparkles	5230		Happy new year	4318
8	(╯°口°)╯(┻━┻	Flipping the table	5742		Crying with laughter	5154		PWS: moving glow sticks for someone	3273
9	ε=ε=(ノ≧∇≦)	Moving forward happily	4997		Year of the Rat	4777		2021 gala show	2528
10	╮(￣▽￣)╭	Joy	4459		Wailing	4198		2233 girls: act cute	1994

Table 1: Top 10 graphicons in the corpus.

Notes: 1) The meanings of most of the kaomojis were derived by referring to the kaomoji dictionary (Kaomoji-Japanese Emoticons, http://kaomoji.ru/en/). The first kaomoji is not found in the dictionary; its meaning was derived from the fact that it is always used together with the Chinese expression 干杯 'cheers/toast'. 2) The kaomojis of Nos. 5, 6, 8 and 9 are a combination of at least two kaomoji elements from the kaomoji dictionary. For example, [°∀°] refers to joy, while [ﾉ] refers to a hand waving to greet someone, suggesting that the meaning of [(°∀°)ﾉ] is greeting happily. 3) PWS in the sticker category is short for Popular Word Series, the meanings of which can be found on the BiliBili platform: https://www.bilibili.com/read/cv4332187

	Kaomoji	Emoji	Sticker
Emotion	70%	30%	20%
Action	50%	40%	40%
Chinese character	0	10%	40%
New Year's celebration	10%	40%	20%
Platform discourse	10%	20%	100%

Table 2: Themes of the top 10 graphicons.

	Kaomoji	Emoji	Sticker
Graph-icon	(⌒▽⌒)	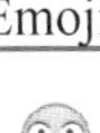	

Table 3: Graphicon evolution for *smile*.

The trajectory from generalized emotion expression to localized platform discourse practices is illustrated by the example of 'smile' in Table 3. The kaomoji represents smile in an abstract and general way, using ⌒ to indicate eyes and ▽ for nose. The emoji smile is different from the smiles on other Chinese social media platforms such as Weibo and WeChat, but still it is somewhat generic and does not encode any platform information. In contrast, the sticker smile is unique to BiliBili, in that it is embedded in the BiliBili icon of a tiny TV set.

Another example is the concept 'wonderful,' which is expressed with a dog face emoji (No. 4 in emojis; see Table 1) but represented by a combination of the Chinese character 妙 and an exclamation point, an example of the Popular Words Series set of stickers (No. 1 in stickers in Table 1). These examples illustrate that the discourse practices of the platform have increasingly been encoded in graphicons.

5 Discussion

5.1 Research questions revisited

We asked how the frequencies of each of the three types of Chinese graphicons are changing over time and what trends are evident from the most frequently-used graphicons of each type. The use of kaomojis shows a clear trajectory of rising to a peak and then declining. Kaomojis have been replaced by emojis and stickers. These results support Konrad et al.'s evolutionary trajectory. It is less clear, however, whether stickers are overtaking emoji in frequency of use on BiliBili; rather, both appear to be on the rise. Moreover, in the last three years (2020-2022), emojis were used with high frequency but with a limited number of types, and it is common to find more than one emoji in a message. As for stickers, there is a decrease in tokens but an increase in types. We propose that frequency of type be included as a criterion for determining which phase a graphicon is currently in.

The trend revealed by the most frequently-used graphicons of each type suggests an evolution from general emotion expression to meanings localized in platform discourse practices. This supports Konrad et al.'s (2020) finding that stickers express more specific meanings than emojis.

We also find an increasing integration of Chinese characters in emojis and stickers. The logographic nature of Chinese characters (Li & Zhu, 2019) makes such integration possible. Though we did not find integration of Chinese characters in the most frequently-used kaomojis, Chinese users in the 1990s were inspired by the practice of using keyboard symbols in kaomojis to create unique graphic representations of Chinese characters for festival celebrations, as shown in the examples in Kozar (1995).

These findings suggest a somewhat different evolutionary trend than that for Western graphicons proposed by Konrad et al. (2020). The types and tokens of emojis and stickers are both on the rise, although stickers do not seem to be overtaking emojis. It is highly possible that emojis have not reached their peak yet. Meanwhile, features of stickers, such as specific references and more detailed graphics, are increasingly being incorporated into emoji design (e.g., the Astonished face in Figure 1). If this trend continues, it is likely to expand the functions of emojis and blur the distinction between emojis and stickers. The icons in the set of Yellow Faces in the GitHub package of BiliBili stickers that we reclassified as emojis (as discussed in Section 3.2) are somewhat ambiguous between the two graphicon types. Meanwhile, the fact that more than one sticker is used per message suggests that users are borrowing from emojis the practice of repeating graphicons in one message. Thus the interrelation of emojis and stickers, as the examples and statistics in this study show, is more complex than one replacing the other.

5.2 Unanticipated findings

Unexpectedly, our results showed different patterns of graphicon usage in comments and replies. More graphicons were used in comments than in replies overall. This finding differs from that of Kaneyasu (2022), who conducted a qualitative study of the use of kaomojis in a Japanese user-generated recipe sharing site. Kaomojis appeared more frequently in replies that were directed at individuals than in comments directed at more general readers. It remains to be explored further using both qualitative and quantitative methods how and why graphicon are used in different ways in comments and replies.

Furthermore, we found that more kaomojis and stickers were used in comments, but the use of emojis was roughly the same in comments and replies. At the moment, we do not have a plausible explanation for this finding, but it at least suggests that certain properties are shared between kaomojis and stickers. This phenomenon also requires further study.

Last, our statistics suggest a "priming effect" of graphicon usage in comments and replies. The use of kaomojis and emojis in replies shows strong correlations with the occurrences of these two types of graphicon in their corresponding comments. Emotion expressions tend to demonstrate priming effects (e.g., Neumann, 2000), but studies about the priming effects of graphicons have focused mainly on the functions of graphicons as primes on language use and processing. For instance, it has been found that emoji primes function as paralanguage to facilitate the processing of relevant emotive linguistic expressions (Yang et al., 2021). Our findings provide evidence that priming is taking place as regards graphicon forms.

6 Conclusion

6.1 Contributions

This paper makes several novel contributions. It presents what we believe is the first longitudinal, comparative study of graphicon use on a Chinese social media platform. It provides support for Konrad et al.'s (2020) evolutionary model concerning the relationship between emoticons (kaomoji) and other graphicons. However, the

BiliBili data do not show stickers leading or taking over from emoji, contrary to Konrad et al.'s intriguing speculation that Chinese graphicons would show that trend. Moreover, our qualitative analysis of the top 10 most frequently used graphicons reveals a trend of graphicon evolution from general emotion expression to meanings localized in the discourse practices of the BiliBili platform.

Further, our analysis of a large longitudinal dataset went beyond reporting overall frequencies of occurrence to explore more fine-grained distinctions between types and tokens and differences in graphicon usage between comments and replies to comments. We also provided statistical evidence for priming effects on graphicon usage in comments and replies. These contributions reveal the complexities of graphicon evolution on BiliBili and generate additional research questions.

6.2 Limitations

A number of limitations potentially affect the generalizability of the patterns of graphicon evolution identified in this study. First, trends in Chinese graphicon usage might differ on a different platform such as WeChat or Weibo, because Chinese social media users are inclined to use platform-specific sets of graphicons. Kaomoji usage is likely more frequent on BiliBili than on any other platform, given that the platform was initially set up to share Japanese anime, comics, and games. Stickers from users' collections cannot be used on BiliBili like they are on WeChat and Weibo. Meanwhile, only a very limited number of sticker sets are free to users, which is likely to have an impact on the varieties of stickers in use. For instance, all of our top 10 stickers are from free sets rather than paid ones. The landscape of sticker usage in WeChat or Weibo, therefore, could be very different. Meanwhile, a majority of BiliBili users are under the age of 35, and this demographic might use graphicons differently from older groups.

Second, our data center on the topic of the Chinese New Year, which is both a strength and a limitation of our study. The topic provided straightforward clues for interpreting the meaning of graphicons, and the fixed content allowed us to focus on graphicon forms. However, while kaomoji meanings are rather general, the denotations of emojis and stickers are increasingly content specific; thus their usage might vary for different topics. We would not expect, for instance, to find as many graphicons on the theme of the Chinese New Year in comments on videos on other topics. More topics, and different platforms, should therefore be analyzed in order to increase the generalizability of our evolutionary findings.

Another factor that might have impacted the evolutionary trajectory is the limited data from 2022. In order to have as much longitudinal data as possible, we included data from 2022; however, these were from only the first two months of the year, so the number of messages from 2022 is relatively small compared with the preceding years. We therefore should be cautious in interpreting the statistics about graphicon usage in 2022, as they might not fully represent the graphicon usage of the year. Follow-up study with future data from BiliBili is needed to develop a fuller picture of graphicon evolution on the platform, particularly with regard to emojis and stickers.

6.3 Future directions

The findings from this study suggest a number of directions for further research. First, a more detailed description of graphicon evolution could be obtained by establishing a relationship between graphicon usage and user demographics such as gender. Second, the differences in graphicon usage between comments and replies could be investigated further by examining the pragmatic functions of the graphicons and their positions in sentences. Qualitative analysis could also shed light on how and why the priming effect takes place in graphicon usage.

Last, as Chinese language features are increasingly integrated with graphicons, it is important to examine the impact of graphicons on textual language and language use. Pavalanathan and Eisenstein (2016) found that creative spelling and typography decreased on Twitter as emoji use increased. We have informally observed a decrease in the use of Chinese words that express attitude on BiliBili as graphicon use has increased over time. This suggests that as graphicons evolve, they are not just supplementing text but are partially replacing it. A study of graphicon frequencies in relation to word frequencies at different points in time could provide empirical evidence in support of this proposition.

Acknowledgments

The authors would like to thank Xixuan Huang, Rongle Tan, and Yanmin Wu for their help with data cleaning, annotation, and analysis. This study was funded by Guangdong Planning Office of Philosophy and Social Science (Grant No. GD21CWY07), and the Department of Education of Guangdong Province (Grant No. 2020WTSCX016).

References

Fathiya Al Rashdi. 2018. Functions of emojis in WhatsApp interaction among Omanis. *Discourse, Context & Media,* 26: 117-126. https://doi.org/10.1016/j.dcm.2018.07.001

Marcel Danesi. 2016. *The Semiotics of Emoji: The Rise of Visual Language in the Age of the Internet*. Bloomsbury Academic, London & New York.

Gabriele de Seta. 2018. Biaoqing: The circulation of emoticons, emoji, stickers, and custom images on Chinese digital media platforms. *First Monday,* 23(9). 10.5210/fm.v23i9.9391

Vyvyan Evans. 2017. *The Emoji Code: The Linguistics behind Smiley Faces and Scaredy Cats*. Picador, New York.

Jing Ge. 2020. The anatomy of memetic stickers: An analysis of sticker competition on Chinese social media. In *Proceedings of the ICWSM Workshops*, pages 1-8. https://doi.org/10.36190/2020.01

Jing Ge and Susan C. Herring. 2018. Communicative functions of emoji sequences on Sina Weibo. *First Monday,* 23(11). http://dx.doi.org/10.5210/fm.v23i11.9413

Susan C. Herring and Ashley Dainas. 2017. "Nice picture comment!" Graphicons in Facebook comment threads. In *Proceedings of The Fiftieth Hawai'i International Conference on System Sciences.* IEEE Press, pages 2185-2194. https://doi.org/10.24251/HICSS.2017.264

Michiko Kaneyasu. 2022. Multimodal strategies for balancing formality and informality: The role of kaomoji in online comment-reply interactions. *Internet Pragmatics,* 5(1): 143-164. https://doi.org/10.1075/ip.00071.kan

Hirofumi Katsuno and Christine R. Yano. 2002. Face to face: on-line subjectivity in contemporary Japan. *Asian Studies Review,* 26(2): 205-231. https://doi.org/10.1111/1467-8403.00025

Artie Konrad, Susan C. Herring, and David Choi. 2020. Sticker and emoji use in Facebook messenger: Implications for graphicon change. *Journal of Computer-Mediated Communication,* 25(3): 217-235. https://doi.org/10.1093/jcmc/zmaa003

Seana Kozar. 1995. Enduring traditions, ethereal transmissions: Recreating Chinese New Year celebrations on the Internet. *Journal of Computer-Mediated Communication,* 1(2). https://doi.org/10.1111/j.1083-6101.1995.tb00329.x

Wei Li and Hua Zhu. 2019. Tranßcripting: playful subversion with Chinese characters. *International Journal of Multilingualism,* 16(2): 145-161. https://doi.org/10.1080/14790718.2019.1575834

Lorenzo Logi and Michele Zappavigna. 2021. A social semiotic perspective on emoji: How emoji and language interact to make meaning in digital messages. *New Media & Society.* https://doi.org/10.1177/14614448211032965

Kris M. Markman and Sae Oshima. 2007. Pragmatic play? Some possible functions of English emoticons and Japanese kaomoji in computer-mediated discourse. *Paper presented at the Association of Internet Researchers Annual Conference 8.0*. Vancouver, Canada.

Daniel C. Molden. 2014. Understanding priming effects in social psychology: An overview and integration. *Social Cognition,* 32(Supplement): 243-249. https://doi.org/10.1521/soco.2014.32.supp.243

Roland Neumann. 2000. The causal influences of attributions on emotions: A procedural priming approach. *Psychological Science,* 11(3): 179-182. https://doi.org/10.1111/1467-9280.00238

Umashanthi Pavalanathan and Jacob Eisenstein. 2016. More emojis, less :) The competition for paralinguistic function in microblog writing. *First Monday,* 22(11). https://doi.org/10.5210/fm.v21i11.6879

Robert R. Provine, Robert J. Spencer, and Darcy L. Mandell. 2007. Emotional expression online: Emoticons punctuate website text messages. *Journal of Language and Social Psychology,* 26(3): 299-307. https://doi.org/10.1177/0261927X06303481

Ya Qin, Guowei Shen, Wenbo Zhao, Yanping Chen, Miao Yu, and Xin Jin. 2019. A network security entity recognition method based on feature template and CNN-BiLSTM-CRF. *Frontiers of Information Technology & Electronic*

Engineering, 20(6): 872-884. https://doi.org/10.1631/FITEE.1800520

Agnese Sampietro. 2019. Emoji and rapport management in Spanish WhatsApp chats. *Journal of Pragmatics,* 143: 109-120. https://doi.org/10.1016/j.pragma.2019.02.009

Ying Tang and Khe Foon Hew. 2018. Emoticon, emoji, and sticker Use in Computer-Mediated Communications: Understanding its communicative function, impact, user behavior, and motive. In L. Deng, W. W. K. Ma, & C. W. R. Fong (Eds.), *New Media for Educational Change*. Springer, Cham. pages 191-201.

Jiayi Yang, Yingxi Yang, Lichao Xiu, and Guoming Yu. 2021. Effect of emoji prime on the understanding of emotional words–evidence from ERPs. *Behavior & Information Technology*: 1-10. https://doi.org/10.1080/0144929X.2021.1874050

Xiaochen Zhang, Weiting Tao, and Sora Kim. 2014. A comparative study on global brands' micro blogs between China and USA: Focusing on communication styles and branding strategies. *International Journal of Strategic Communication,* 8(4): 231-249. https://doi.org/10.1080/1553118X.2014.886251

Yiqiong Zhang, Min Wang, and Ying Li. 2021. More than playfulness: Emojis in the comments of a WeChat official account. *Internet Pragmatics,* 4(2): 247-271. https://doi.org/10.1075/ip.00048.zha

Author Index